LIFE EVERLASTING

A Course of Sermons

BY

MOST REV. TIHAMER TOTH

TRANSLATED BY

V. G. AGOTAI

EDITED BY

REV. NEWTON THOMPSON, S.T.D.

B. HERDER BOOK CO.

15 & 17 SOUTH BROADWAY, ST LOUIS, MO.

AND

33 QUEEN SQUARE, LONDON, W. C.

1952

NIHIL OBSTAT

Sti. Ludovici, die 20. Sept., 1940

F. J. Holweck,

Censor Librorum

IMPRIMATUR

Sti. Ludovici, die 21. Sept., 1940

✠ *Joannes J. Glennon,*

Archiepiscopus

CONTENTS

CHAPTER   PAGE

   I. BELIEF IN LIFE EVERLASTING 1

  II. EXISTENCE OF THE SOUL 12

 III. THE TEACHING OF RELIGION 24

  IV. REASONABLENESS OF BELIEF IN LIFE EVERLASTING . . 35

   V. FRUIT OF BELIEF IN LIFE EVERLASTING 48

  VI. THE GATE OF LIFE EVERLASTING 60

 VII. DEATH VICTORIOUS 71

VIII. DEATH THE TEACHER 84

  IX. THE WARNING OF DEATH 97

   X. THE SOBERING FACT OF DEATH 108

  XI. DEATH THE GUIDE 119

 XII. DEATH THE COMFORTER 129

XIII. DEATH THE VANQUISHED 142

 XIV. PURGATORY 154

  XV. ETERNAL PERDITION 167

 XVI. ETERNAL BLISS 181

      INDEX 195

I

BELIEF IN LIFE EVERLASTING

THIS declaration is not only the conclusion of our Creed and crown of our belief, but also its foundation and support. "I believe in the resurrection of the body and life everlasting." With this triumphant assurance the Christian Creed ends. On this also the whole Christian religion is erected.

Life everlasting. What a promise and hope beyond imagination! Unsurpassed bliss! How much encouragement, how much consolation, how much strength and energy emanate from this belief!

Life everlasting. If there really is life everlasting, then it is not such a dreadful tragedy, that my earthly life is continual pain and suffering. If there is life everlasting, then it is not such an insupportable burden, that I have to live my earthly life misunderstood and unloved. If there is life everlasting, then I am not appalled that death should deprive me of this earthly life. If there is life everlasting, then in this earthly life only one thing is important: to insure by my present life that blissful life everlasting. O yes, if there is life everlasting.

But what if there is none?

Is it certain that there is? Can we say the last words of the Creed with absolute certainty: "I believe in life everlasting"? Is this not a mere fancy? Is it not a deceptive dream? An unfounded longing?

I should now like to consider the problem of life everlasting in all its details because in this way earthly life will be seen in quite another light, and its every manifestation will gain quite a different meaning.

The King of eternal life, our blessed heavenly Father, grant that in the souls of all who reflect with us upon the question of life everlasting, this belief may become unfaltering. And may He grant that we attain a blissful eternity by the goodness of our earthly lives so that the inscription on the tombstone of a great French Catholic writer, Louis Veuillot (1813–1883), composed by himself before his death, may be applicable to all of us.

> When I have breathed my last in prayer,
> A cross erect upon my grave;
> And on my tombstone write these words:
> "He lived believing; now he knows."

I

THE IMPORTANCE OF THE QUESTION

A. If we consider the history of the human mind, we see that since earliest times two opposing views of life have divided mankind into two main groups.

1) These two groups are so opposed to each other that they can never hope to reach an agreement.

"Enjoy yourself to the fullest, for life is short and after it there is nothing." This is the motto of one group. "What doth it profit a man if he gain the whole world and suffer the loss of his own soul?" (Matt. 16: 26.) This is the motto of the other. And all of us must decide which motto to choose.

Our decision—on which side to take our stand—will affect our whole life. If there is no world to come, no eternal life, then we are foolish to deny ourselves anything whatever on this earth. If there is no world hereafter, then let us enjoy this brief span of earthly life to the utmost. St. Paul said: "If in this life only we have hope in Christ, we are of all men most miserable" (I Cor. 15: 19). On the other hand, if we look forward to a world to come and a life everlasting, we must do everything to attain life: that everlasting life, that blissful everlasting life.

2) The great Pascal was right when he said: "The immortality of the soul is so important, it touches us so deeply, that we cannot remain indifferent to this question unless we have lost all interest in life. According as we have or have not hope of eternal blessings, all our acts and thoughts are directed into such divergent channels that in all common sense we cannot pursue our way without determining its direction from this highest point of view."

This is indeed the one and only decisive question for all men: Is there a world to come or is there none? A decisive question which we cannot evade. We cannot do what a certain soldier did who, poor fellow, had not learned to pray at home. But on the battlefield, amid a hail of bullets, he began to pray thus: "Dear God (if there is a God), save my soul (if I have a soul) that I may not go to hell (if there is a hell) but to heaven (if there is a heaven)." No, dear brethren, we cannot do this. We must all choose: Is there life everlasting or is there not?

B. How different our whole life will be if we believe in the hereafter; and how different it will be if we do not believe!

1) How different this earthly life will be! If we believe that this life is only a beginning and that before God's judgment seat the continuation of it awaits us, then there are no more insoluble life problems for us, earthly injustice does not crush us, we can endure even the hardest struggles. Yes, this earthly life has a purpose only if it has a continuation in life everlasting.

But if we do not believe in the next world? Then, like a thousand sphinxes, disaster and trials and sickness and death will grin at us in this life. Without belief in a life hereafter, our present life is unbearable torment. It is like a runaway locomotive rushing along the rails without any goal, until somewhere it plunges off the tracks and comes to a sudden and disastrous stop. Consider man as an immortal creature, and everything about him becomes great, everything is understandable. But take him as a being without immortal destiny, and dark clouds envelop his aimless paths.

2) If we believe in life everlasting, how different death is from what it is if we do not believe!

Death comes to the unbeliever as well as to the believer; but in the death of the two is all the difference between earth and heaven. The unbeliever clutches frantically at fleeting life with a pitiable, hopeless, spasmodic gesture of his trembling fingers. And the believer? As he approaches the end of his life, he becomes calmer and quieter; in his last confession he once more sets in order his account with almighty God and thus awaits the last solemn moment.

In the year 1890 when the great English convert, Cardinal Newman, felt that death was imminent, he sent everybody from his room with these words: "I can meet my end alone." What faith, what strength, what will-power! It is a real "euthanasia," "a good death," when we can say with the psalmist: "Though I should walk in the midst of the shadow of death, I will fear no evils, for Thou art with me" (Ps. 22: 4).

"Hail, brother Death," St. Francis of Assisi cried triumphantly when he was told that he had not long to live. Truly above such a deathbed the tender light of the life to come already dawns gently, the light that makes Murillo's famous picture, "The death of St. Clare," so touchingly beautiful.

Dante once wrote that "life is a hastening toward death" (*Purgatorio,* canto 23). This is true: life is continual death; only in the last hour of life do we cease to die. This last moment comes also to him who has not believed in life everlasting. But, alas, then he is overtaken by "the deathbed tragedy" of which Jean Paul speaks. Because in that hour such a man fares as does a speculator on the Stock Exchange, who takes the latest report into his hand after a sharp decline in stocks, and is startled to see that all his shares have become worthless.

3) How different is our consolation in affliction if we believe in life everlasting! Sometimes consolation is utterly empty, banal. "I also had a mother, she died, too." Is this a consolation for us? Or: "Time will ease your sorrow." "We shall not forget her memory." "His death was so peaceful; he just fell asleep." No, no! Only the belief in life everlasting consoles us: that our dear one continues to live and that we shall see each other again. Thus we feel that "blessed are they that mourn"—that mourn like this—"for they shall be comforted" (Matt. 5:5).

O yes, this is consolation. How truly the renowned physicist of the past century, Robery Maye, writes: "A strong, scientifically founded faith in the individual continuation of the life of the soul and of the direction of human destiny by a higher power was my greatest comfort when I held the cold hand of my dying mother between my hands."

This is surely the truest philosophy of life: to appraise life from the viewpoint of death, and to view death by the light of life everlasting. Thus death becomes life's great regulator. To the sad and afflicted it says: Be patient; it will not last much longer. To the frivolous it says: Beware, everything comes to an end quickly. To the arrogant boaster it says:

Only wait; you will soon see what becomes of you. And to the conscientious struggler it says: Endure; in the end you will gain the reward of virtue.

After this, dear brethren, I need not further discuss whether our question is important or not.

II

MANKIND'S BELIEF IN A FUTURE LIFE

Let us note the interesting fact that never has a people lived on this earth, that did not believe in a future life.

A. However far back, even into prehistoric times, scholarly investigation extends, where we find traces of man we also find evidence of his belief in a life beyond the grave. What aroused this belief in a life after death? Undoubtedly the word of God resounding in the human soul. And what nourished this belief? The countless imperfections, injustices, and miseries of earthly life, to which only the perfection of eternal life can give the solution.

The extensive labor expended on the preparation of the tombs of prehistoric man speaks eloquently of this belief. Prehistoric man did not regard a corpse merely as something loathsome, to be hurriedly cast by the wayside and left to itself; on the contrary, it was an object of reverent care. That they lacked a clear idea of the soul and did not reflect upon it with the knowledge possessed by Christians, does not militate against the fact that the most primitive peoples believed in the reality of life after death. Therefore they placed food and weapons in the graves and sometimes killed the wives and slaves of the dead, that there should be someone to serve them in the next world.

B. If we consider the great historic races, we find every-

where belief in a life after death, of course in various and
sometimes fantastic forms.

The Egyptian pyramids, sarcophagi, and inscriptions, prepared with much care and artistic feeling, speak of this belief.
The Babylonian memorials, and the Olympus and Tartarus
of the Greeks, speak of this, too.

"Death ends everything? What a pagan way of speaking,"
we say. But it is not a pagan way of speaking; the pagans
did not speak like that.

Listen to Socrates reply when his friend Crito questions
him before his death: "Have you any wish that we can fulfil? How shall we bury you?" "What do you say?" replied
Socrates. "You will bury me? You can bury my body. But me
you cannot bury." This reply calls to mind what is written
on the cross on Gardonyi's grave in the citadel at Eger: "Only
the body."

Cicero wrote a whole book on the immortality of the soul
(*De immortalitate animae*). In one of his other works he
reasons, with psychological insight, in this manner: "The
greatest proof that nature herself silently acknowledges immortality is that the question of what will come after death,
lies close to everyone's heart, indeed it lies very close to everyone's heart. . . . I wonder what all our great men can have
thought, those great men who died for their country? Did
they think that at the end of their earthly lives even their
names would disappear? Without the hope of a continuation
of life after death, not one of them would have died for his
country. . . . Rooted in the soul, somehow or other, is the
premonition, who would be so foolish as to live in continual
weariness and among continual dangers? If, on the one hand,
the general opinion is the voice of nature, and on the other
hand, everyone in the world is agreed that there is something

that has reference to those who have departed this life, then we ought to make this opinion our own" (*Tusc. Disp.*, I, 14). Are these not interesting words from pre-Christian times?

C. We find the same opinion among the people living today. It is a fact well established, that we do not find a single people without a belief that death is but a gateway beyond which life in some form continues. If we consider the most distant peoples—the Lapps, the Eskimos, the Hottentots, the Zulus, the Patagonians—we find that each believes this truth in some form: on this earth we are pilgrims toward another home, where we shall live eternally.

Today we often hear that the Chinese are the least religious people in the world. But among them belief in life after death is so strong that almost their entire religion is connected with veneration for the spirits of deceased ancestors.

The sensual Mohammedan and the pious native of India, the highly educated Greek and the materialistic Roman, the primitive Teuton and the barbarous Scythian, the serious American Indian and the lighthearted South Sea Islander, the hot-blooded negro and the hardheaded Australian, the despised Hottentot and the uncivilized Fuegian: all of them believe in a future life and look forward to a reunion in the world to come.

What has ever been the universal belief of mankind springs from the depths of the human soul; it is the result of the primitive philosophy of the human mind.

No one can rightly object that for a long time mankind believed that the sun revolves round the earth. Man did, indeed, believe this, because his senses testified that such was the case; his senses deceived him. But when man believes in a future life, he believes *despite his senses:* he believes although his senses tell him nothing of all this; on the contrary, they seem opposed to it.

III

IS THERE A WORLD BEYOND?

We can, however, go still further with this argument.

A. Let us suppose, although it is not so, but let us suppose that we who believe in the next world cannot support our belief with stronger arguments than the arguments adduced by those who deny it. For the moment let us suppose that both assertions are equally uncertain and that, not even by a hairsbreadth, is it more certain that there is life everlasting than that there is none. Now I ask: Does not human wisdom demand that I should rather take my stand for belief in the world to come? Is it not wiser to reckon with a danger, even if it never happens, than to ignore it although it may happen?

People insure themselves against many things, do they not? They insure against fire. Do they insure because their house will certainly be burnt down? Of course not. They take out an insurance policy because their house may burn down, and in that case it is well for them to have it insured. They insure against accidents, against hail-storms, against theft. Are they certain that an accident will happen to them, that hail will damage their crops, that burglars will break into their house? No. But these things may happen.

Well, dear brethren, if we were in this position with regard to the next world: it may be that there is one, it may be that there is none—we are not, in fact, in this position; but let us suppose that we are—then would not sober common sense demand that we live our lives as though there were a world to come?

B. You must allow me to reason in such a very material way, because some people are impressed only by such arguments.

Let us take the worst case: I have lived as if there were a world beyond. I have taken great care of my morals, of my honor. Then I die. And then, in fact, there is nothing after this life. What have I lost? At best, I have lost the very doubtful joys of sinful earthly pleasures; but even then I have enjoyed the exalting sensation that accompanies one on the path of honor. If, on the other hand, there is a world to come, then I have gained everything.

Now let us take the other case: I have lived as if there were no world beyond, frivolously sipping life's sinful pleasures. I die. And it appears that really there is nothing beyond the grave. What have I gained? The long-forgotten deceptive joys of sinful pleasure. But if it appears that there is a world to come? What have I lost then? Everything! Everything! Forever!

"Dear Christian, how deceived you are, if heaven is a fairy tale," an unbeliever once said mockingly to a believer. But the latter replied: "O, dear atheist, how deceived you are, if hell is no fairy tale."

Yes, brethren, to live honestly is the smallest loss and the greatest gain. But to live in sin is the smallest gain and the greatest loss. Then ought we not to take our stand for the world to come, even if our arguments for it were as weak as the arguments of those that deny it?

But such is not the case. That death is not the terminus of life, but only a gateway through which we must pass and beyond which a more beautiful, more colorful, never-ending life awaits us, is equally witnessed to by the general conviction of mankind, by man's reasoning mind, and by divine revelation. So many and such strong arguments testify to this that we should have to deny the ability of the human mind to recognize truth, were we to doubt the reality of life beyond the grave.

My dear brethren. Ever since man has lived upon the earth he has always striven to prolong his life, if only by a short span. With what passionate eagerness he sought the elixir that would give him unending life! A Chinese legend relates that a certain emperor built a tower reaching to the skies; on the roof of the tower he erected a golden staff with a golden cup on its tip. With the clear dew thus gathered, he mixed a powder that was composed of precious jewels. He then drank this mixture, in the expectation that he would never die. What a vain experiment! What a foolish endeavor!

How much research has been undertaken by man in the study of this question! We have striven to know how we should nourish ourselves, how we should clothe ourselves, how we should construct our houses, how we should regulate our daily lives, merely that we may live longer. Yet, after all our endeavors, we have not been able to save our lives from the grave. Today the words of Job are still true: "Man born of a woman, living for a short time, is filled with many miseries. Who cometh forth like a flower and is destroyed and fleeth as a shadow" (Job 14: 1 f.).

Yet there is one marvelous and quite certain "life-lengthener," if I may coin a word, not valid for a few years only or for a hundred or for a million, but forever: our holy Christian faith.

Non omnis morior ("I do not die entirely") said the great Latin poet Horace, writing of his own literary fame. But what he meant with regard only to his fame, we feel in the instinctive desire of all mankind for immortality, for life. I do not die entirely. I shall live after death. I believe in the resurrection of the body. I believe in life everlasting. Amen.

II

EXISTENCE OF THE SOUL

The Catholic Creed concludes with these triumphant words: "I believe in the resurrection of the body and life everlasting." With the most unwavering firmness, we Catholics believe in the next life. Let us see upon what grounds we believe. What arguments support our contention? On two subsequent occasions we shall consider what Divine revelation and human reason have to say. But today let us examine the assertions of those who deny life everlasting because they deny that man has a soul.

Do some people, really, not believe in the existence of a soul?

Are there some whose faces are turned always earthward? Whose eyes are blindfolded, as it were? Who wander so hopelessly and aimlessly? And are such people to be found in large numbers?

Half a century ago such an attitude was common. At that time a benumbing tendency, that of materialism, held sway in natural science, in physics, unwilling to acknowledge anything in the world except matter, and endeavoring to explain everything in terms of matter. "There is no soul, only matter," was the refrain. "What until now has been called soul and spiritual phenomena consists of nothing but matter's most subtle manifestations. What is not material, does not exist. Therefore what we cannot perceive with our senses, that is, what we should have to believe, does not exist."

At that time the world resounded with such assertions.

Since then, however, much water has flowed under the bridges; and materialism, as a world-philosophy, belongs to the things of the past. That beside the material world—measurable, perceptible, and tangible to our senses—a wonderfully rich spiritual world also exists, transcending the material, is today denied only by those whose knowledge has remained on the plane of half a century ago.

But I am sorry to say, some such people may still be found. Now and then you may hear a remark about life everlasting that plainly comes from the rusty arsenal of materialism. To-day, then, we will consider that science does not deny the existence of the soul, and that sound reasoning demands its existence.

I

THE ATTITUDE OF SCIENCE

Whoever asserts anything, may rightly be required to prove his assertion. Christianity asserts the existence of a world to come, a life beyond the grave. We shall see how many arguments there are to support this assertion. But what arguments are adduced by those who deny the existence of such a world?

Those who deny a future life generally refer to "science" with a superior gesture. "Belief in the existence of the soul and of a life beyond the grave is in opposition to science," they say with abounding self-confidence.

A. Surely we may ask them to tell us which science it is that contradicts this doctrine of our faith, that the human soul is immortal. Which science does this?

1) Perhaps the science of law? If the soul is immortal, if there is life after death, then do the laws of justice collapse, or do they not receive their highest sanction precisely through this belief?

2) Or philosophy? Perhaps by denial of life hereafter, we may more easily solve the enigmas of the world? Great truths, felt instinctively, seen clearly, considered certain, although man cannot prove them, lie latent within him. In this way he senses immortality. Mankind unanimously believes in life after death, although it cannot prove this by mathematical methods.

If, indeed, the belief in immortality, this belief which is rooted in the depths of the human heart, that immortality for which we yearn most eagerly from childhood to the grave, if this belief is nothing but a fancy, a fairy tale, and not truth, then no truth is to be found on earth.

3) Which science contradicts the belief in life everlasting? History? Mathematics? What law opposes the continued life of the soul? Someone replies: "Natural science. Natural science has proved that man consists of a body only; he has no soul. What we commonly call spiritual phenomena are nothing but functions of the brain. If, therefore, man has no soul, nothing is there to live on after the death of the body."

Those "modern" people who today still argue that biology can explain every spiritual phenomenon by the material processes of the body and that therefore man has no soul, do not realize that they are not at all modern and up-to-date, that they are behind the times. People spoke that way a few decades ago, at a time when a flood of material misconception denying the soul's existence inundated the scientific world. But let us, by way of example, quote a few lines from a recent number of an esteemed medical periodical (*Jo egeszseg,* 1931, pp. 191 f.).

"Let us imagine that science already enables us to look into the living, functioning brain and that we can not only measure its temperature but, in consequence of some wonderful progress made by science, we can also make the brain's molecular movements visible or at least calculable, and so take delight in observing their order and harmony. Even in such an event, however marvelous the sight would be, in no part of it could we find thought itself. We might possibly see vibrations, the change of position made by the molecules, the order of different movements, but thoughts, feelings, desires, plans, and the active, colorful life of the soul itself we could not see. Nor anything that even distantly resembles it. The anatomy of the brain does not show even a trace of thought."

And the same periodical continues: "According to Claude Bernard, the famous biologist, to assert that thought is a secretion of the brain, signifies just as much as if one were to say 'time is a secretion of the clock.'

"If the ego were nothing more than a mass of brain, if thought, determination, project, enthusiasm, joy, sorrow, judgment, knowledge, art, poetry, were nothing but biological circular motions of the atoms of the brain, then science would know which group of brain molecules thinks, which chemical group of atoms feels, which plans, which judges, which fears, which rejoices. In no way can anyone show how an immaterial spiritual something, such as thought and the entire colorful and variable spiritual life, originates from mere matter."

Yes, this is the up-to-date scientific way of thinking. We will now examine how thinking man came to this conclusion.

II

THE ATTITUDE OF REASON

"No life exists beyond the grave because, after the death of the body, nothing remains to live; no such thing as a soul exists. No one has ever yet held a soul in his hand. Man has not a soul; only a brain. What we call soul is the functioning of the brain. A child's brain is small: its thoughts are also small. A man's brain is diseased: his thoughts are also sickly. A man's brain is old: his thoughts are also old. A man's brain dies: his thinking also dies." Those who deny the existence of the soul argue thus and do not realize how many errors they have uttered in one breath.

"No one has ever yet held a soul in his hand." Well, well, have you ever held a sunbeam in your hand? Have you ever held truth in your hand? Have you ever held an electric current in your hand?

"I have never actually held an electric current in my hand," you may say, "but I feel that it exists, because it heats and lights, and gives me a shock; I do not see the current, indeed, but I perceive its functioning."

Ah, then we are on the right path. Neither do we actually see the soul, but we perceive its functioning. That man is able to think and to will is a complete refutation of the arguments brought forward by those who deny the existence of the soul.

A. First, man's thinking faculty refutes them. Brain is soul, they say.

1) But what is brain? A mass of matter that can be weighed on the scales. And what is thought? What is love, enthusiasm, virtue, anger, sin, and the many other manifestations that we call the function of the soul? A spiritual something. Now solve the riddle if you can: how can matter bring the spiritual into existence? Who that denies the soul can answer this?

There is no spiritual soul in us, only matter. Then who understands our spiritual thinking faculty? If I fill a sack with matter, let us say with apples or with potatoes, however large the sack it will at length be full and will hold nothing more, because it is matter. But my soul, my thinking faculty, can receive impressions of the external world into itself without limit, and it will never be full, because it is not matter.

During the functions of my soul in earthly life it has need of my body as of an implement. On the other hand, it has reflective functions that cannot be explained as mere processes of matter. Who can explain, in material terms, the abstract and universal concepts, during the creation of which the soul completely withdraws from things perceptible to the senses, and forms universal ideas that cannot be found in reality? Or when it establishes laws that are valid in the material world, but that have nothing material about them. I even construct entire branches of science—for instance, mathematics—that are of an altogether immaterial nature. Man is able to do this only because in him lives a soul that is not matter, but spirit. I confess I could never believe—yet those who deny the existence of the spiritual soul must believe—that, for instance, when Michelangelo created his matchless statue of Moses or designed the cupola of St. Peter's, only his hand, his pencil, and his chisel were at work. Only these, and nothing more. On the contrary, I believe that a much more important work was accomplished by the artist's soul that conceived and worked out the idea of the masterpiece.

2) My logical thinking faculty raised me above all the creatures of earth. How magnificent are the brilliant stars on a quiet summer evening! But a single human thought is worth more than a whole galaxy of stars. Only man, this little part of the universe, creates abstract ideas, rises in thought to transcendental heights, and reflects upon the infinite. Yet he could not think of the infinite unless something infinite lived in him, his soul; just as the eye could not perceive light unless it were created for light.

3) "We have no soul, only a brain." How this is disproved

by human consciousness! If it were true, then man could not utter that magnificent, enigmatical, immeasurably profound word "I." The conscious sense of the ego, self-consciousness, designates man as a person and raises him above every other creature of earth.

How much time we might spend in reflecting on this little word "I"! Who is this "I" in me? Does my head think? No. But I think. Does my heart love? No. But I love. Who is this I? Has anyone seen it? No. No one. Has anyone heard it? No one. Yet it exists. From whom is it? From whom is this mysterious I in me? From the eternal I who said of Himself: "I am who am" (Ex. 3: 14), that is, whose essence is "to be."

The "I" is always the same in me, yesterday, years and years ago, therefore every conscious phenomenon in me must have a permanent basis. This feeling of the "I" is something of the consciousness that cannot be explained away by nerves and brain-substance.

4) "But without the brain there is no spiritual functioning," you may be told. And this is true in this earthly life. The brain plays the part of a telephone exchange. Every nerve leads to it, and there sits the operator that receives and sums up impressions. But in the telephone system, the wire is not what produces the thoughts, the conversations that pass over it. If the wire is faulty, the functioning of the telephone is faulty, too. Even though the operator may be sitting in the exchange, you cannot telephone. Nor can you if the operator leaves the exchange, even though the apparatus remains there. In like manner if our soul leaves our body, no longer will any thought be there, yet the brain remains where it was.

You see this little instrument before me. It is the microphone into which I am now speaking. An electric current runs through it, receives my every word, and broadcasts it into the ether. The microphone is the brain, I am the soul.

Brain is needed, the soul also is needed. But if this micro-phone is damaged, then I should speak in vain; no one outside the church would hear my words. I cannot communicate my thoughts to it. But can I say that the thoughts you now hear expressed are manufactured by the microphone? Most de-cidedly not.

Just so I cannot reach my distant listeners without the mi-crophone. If the microphone is impaired, let us say if it is "ill," they may hear my voice, but only faintly or accompanied by crackling noises. So if a man's brain is decrepit or ill, then it is able to transmit the soul's thoughts only in a faulty man-ner. On the other hand, even a healthy brain is useless if the soul leaves it; just as the best microphone might be here, but if I go away from it, it will not transmit my voice. With poor tools not even the best sculptor can work well: nor can he without any tools at all. Yet who would say that the tool is the artist? But that is what is said by those who declare that brain is soul.

"But you know," someone may say, "the behavior of these infantile, sickly, or aged brains still confuses me. The train of thought of these persons with undeveloped brains or with brains that have become diseased, is so foolish and sickly that we must explain everything with the brain. Where is the soul in these cases?"

Yet it is there, my brethren: a normal soul, not infantile or sickly human soul, is there. But it cannot express itself. Listen to this analogy. Two persons are seated in the same room. The one has the ear pieces of a simple detector radio-receiver on his head; in front of the other stands a six-tube super-radio. The room is full of the waves of hundreds and hun-dreds of broadcasting stations which knock and ask for ad-mittance at both apparatuses. The one who has a delicate receiving apparatus hears many of them; but the man with the crude detector sits there and hears nothing of the whole colorful mass of sound; at most he may hear a local station. Why does he hear nothing else? Because his receiving apparatus is weak. The infantile, undeveloped, or diseased brain can be compared to a weak radio receiver. There beside it is the transmitter, a soul neither infantile nor diseased; but it transmits the most beautiful programs in vain if no machine is at hand to receive them.

B. The contention of those who deny the existence of the soul is refuted, and the spirituality of the soul, that is, its immortality, is proved by its spontaneous activity.

1) Man is capable of willing in opposition to his desires of a material nature. He is able to renounce what his senses eagerly desire, and he is able to do what his whole material being protests against. This splendid privilege is the true charter of man. Therefore we honor especially those who practice this, because from this issue humanity's most beautiful virtues: unselfishness, loyal friendship, self-sacrificing love toward one's fellow man and one's country. As long as these virtues flourish on earth we shall always have decisive proof that the soul is not matter, but more than matter, different from matter: spirit. If the soul were matter, if matter constituted the essence of the soul, then all this would be impossible: the soul could not act in opposition to its own nature.

We feel: the soul in us is one thing, and the body another. Or are they not different? From where, then, comes my self-reproach if I have done wrong? Is it not from the soul? Whence comes a feeling of sadness even when I have satisfied all my material needs and my body is suffering no ailment? Is it not from the soul?

2) "Man has no soul, only brain." But then I should have to believe an impossibility, namely, that all general abstract ideas and all the moral decisions that I make in opposition to

matter, are of material origin. Then I must believe that the prodigious will power of a Caesar, a Charlemagne, a Napoleon, the genius of a Michelangelo, a Raphael, a Leonardo da Vinci, the world-encompasing spiritual strength of an Aristotle and of a St. Thomas, the self-immolating love for humanity of a St. Francis of Assisi and of a St. Elizabeth—that all this is nothing but the vibration of material atoms. I must believe that the soldier's dauntless love of country, that the self-sacrificing vigil of a mother beside her child's sickbed, that all holy enthusiasm and performance of duty is nothing but the dance of corporeal molecules, their mingling and electrical vibration.

3) "Man has no soul, only brain." Then what evolves the marvelous strength that enables a dying person to keep himself alive sometimes for hours, or even for days? Who has not heard of cases which are clear signs that the soul kept life in the body that had already begun to die. I read of a mother whose death was imminent, but she did not want to die until her two sons had arrived, the one from the distant North, the other from the South. They arrived, and ten minutes later her heart ceased to beat. Who can explain this if man has no soul?

4) "Man has no soul, only brain." Then who can explain the not uncommon phenomenon, that persons who have been out of their minds for many years, regain their sanity shortly before death? This is a well-known fact in medical science. It is perhaps sufficient if I mention one famous case, the mother of Emperor Charles V, "mad" Johanna, whose brain was clouded for forty-nine years; on the day of her death, April 5, 1555, she entirely recovered her senses and died with a prayer on her lips. To recover one's senses just when the brain is steadily becoming weaker, is possible only if the brain is not all, but the soul, and this soul at the moment of death

frees itself from the fetters of matter and in its functioning has no more need of matter.

This is explicable only if we believe that all these phenomena are the first signs of life of the soul preparing to leave the chrysalis of the body, and first movement in the egg of the little bird preparing for flight, which must first break the shell of the egg that it may achieve this new form of life.

There is an empiric truth in the words of Victor Hugo: "You say that the soul is only the expression of bodily forces. But then how comes it that my soul becomes more radiant as my bodily forces prepare to leave me?" Truly, who could understand what so frequently happens, that the bodily life and bodily force of the dying often give evidence in the final moments of surprising, perhaps till then unknown, spiritual abilities?

If Socrates could say that the beginning of philosophy is to know that we know nothing, then today we could add that the conclusion of philosophy is to know that we must believe.

My dear brethren. Today's sermon was intended in the first place for those who do not believe in eternal life. But is it not an interesting fact that not even such persons can free themselves from the thought of life beyond the grave? Nor can those who would gladly do so. Nor even those who say that they do not concern themselves with this question.

Because this is a question that cannot leave anyone unconcerned. It is a question that springs from the innermost depths of the soul: What becomes of us after death? Is everything annihilated or does something of us remain? Is death the end of life, or the beginning of a new life?

How right Plato is when he makes the dying Socrates say to those around him: "It is truly worthy of man's remembrance. If the soul is immortal then we must provide not only for the span of this earthly life, but for all time, and only then does the danger of neglecting the soul appear in all its dreadfulness. If in any case death meant parting from everything, then to die would be gain to the wicked man because by doing so he would be parted from his body, his soul, and also from his wickedness. However, as the soul appears to be immortal, there is for him no other escape from evil, than the endeavor to be as good and as sensible as possible. For the soul takes no other property with it to the next world than the self-discipline it has expended upon itself, with which it nourished itself and of which we assert that immediately upon the arrival of the deceased it will be of the greatest advantage or harm to him." What noble words from the lips of a genius who did not know the light of Christ! Amen.

THE TEACHING OF RELIGION ABOUT LIFE EVERLASTING

CHRISTIANITY has a joyful, triumphant word that often recurs in the liturgy. This word is "Alleluia." Alleluia! Praise the Lord! Rejoice!

Whence comes this triumphant fervor? From the fact that Christianity is the religion of victory. In Christianity love has overcome hate, belief unbelief, the Son of God sin, and, what perhaps gives us most cause for rejoicing, life has overcome death. Alleluia! Rejoice, for life has overcome death!

We all die. No difference of opinion exists about that. But what comes afterward? This is the starting-point of discussion. That the great Swiss artist, Böcklin, painted his picture "The Isle of the Dead" from the uttermost depths of human sorrow, is acknowledged by everyone. But somehow we feel that in spite of all its artistic value the picture is incomplete, something is lacking.

We acknowledge that this picture makes one shudder. A steep rock rises defiantly out of the sea, like inevitable fate. A few cypresses stand dolefully upon it. In the wall of the rock yawn the mouths of caves: the dwelling-places of death. Black clouds lower in the heavens. The waves murmur as if in unceasing lament. A small boat is just arriving at the shore; it brings a coffin; a white-shrouded figure bends reverently over the coffin. And the black mouths of the yawning chasms seem to say: Today this one has come to us. Tomorrow will come another. And some day you will come. Quite surely you will also come.

Truly a startling picture, an artistic painting, yet in some way deficient. Something is lacking in it. What is there behind the cave's mouth and what awaits us after death? This is lacking.

And here the immense superiority of Christianity is seen when it proclaims with triumphant certainty that behind the sad Isle of the Dead the ocean of life everlasting awaits us.

The thought of eternal life was not first given to the world by Christianity. With the infallible power of Jesus' words, Christianity strengthened and exalted to unconditional certainty the desire and longing and instinctive premonition that has always dwelt in man about the continuation of earthly life, about the new form of life that follows upon death.

In today's sermon let us consider what Christianity teaches about life everlasting. Let us see how our Lord proclaimed eternal life, and how the idea of God is surety for it.

I

THE TEACHING OF CHRIST

We turn the pages of the Gospel. Not one thought do we find reiterated so many times and in so many different ways as the doctrine of life everlasting, the belief in the world to come. From this thought Christ starts out, and to this He returns. One thought is the basis of His every teaching: Save thy soul. But why, if there is no hereafter?

A. Let us examine our Lord's teaching, let us see how many times and with what emphasis He repeats that this earthly life is only a beginning, only a time of probation, only a preface, but the book itself comes in life everlasting.

1) How varied our Lord's words about this life everlasting!

"Be you also ready, because at what hour you know not the Son of man will come" (Matt. 24: 4). "Watch ye therefore because you know not the day nor the hour" (Matt. 25: 13). But why should we be prepared and why should we watch if with death there is an end to everything?

"Labor not for the meat which perisheth, but for that which endureth unto life everlasting" (John 6: 27). "If any man eat of this bread, he shall live forever" (John 6: 52).

"Wide is the gate and broad is the way that leadeth to destruction, and many there are who go in thereat. How narrow is the gate and strait is the way that leadeth to life, and few there are that find it" (Matt. 7: 13, 14).

Here are the Savior's words emanating a profound love: "God so loved the world as to give His only begotten Son, that whosoever believeth in Him may not perish, but may have life everlasting" (John 3: 16).

Let us note how He prepares His Apostles for persecutions: "Fear ye not them that kill the body, and are not able to kill the soul; but rather fear him that can destroy both soul and body in hell" (Matt. 10: 28).

We know what He promised on the cross to the repentant thief: "This day thou shalt be with Me in paradise" (Luke 23: 43).

And let us hear His great promise to each of us: "He that eateth My flesh and drinketh My blood hath everlasting life, and I will raise him up in the last day" (John 6: 55).

How many listen uncomprehendingly to these words! I will raise him up. The dead will live? Is this possible? Is it not an audacious exaggeration? How many shrug their shoulders unbelievingly! How many laugh at Christ for saying them!

Laugh at Him? During His lifetime they once laughed at Him. When He bent over Jairus' dead daughter, saying to the mourners who were rending their clothes and weeping in impotent despair: "Why make you this ado and weep? The damsel is not dead, but sleepeth. And they laughed Him to scorn" (Mark 5: 41), and she arose and walked.

See how often and in how many ways Christ taught that there is a continuation of earthly life, there is life everlasting.

2) The same thing is taught by His parables, one more beautiful than the other, and by His similitudes.

The laborers wished to uproot the cockle that grew among the wheat, but the goodman said they should leave it until the harvest, then reap it and burn it (Matt. 13: 30).

The fishermen sorted the fish in their nets and threw away the worthless ones. "So shall it be at the end of the world; the angels shall go out and shall separate the wicked from among the just" (Matt. 13: 49).

On another occasion a rich man speaks to his steward thus: "Give an account of thy stewardship" (Luke 16: 12).

The bridegroom says to the five foolish virgins: "I know you not" (Matt. 25: 12).

Christ says to His faithful servant: "Well done, good and faithful servant . . . enter thou into the joy of thy Lord" (Matt. 25: 21).

If we sum up all this, we can truly say that our Lord's whole mission, His entire life, His suffering, and His death are built upon the belief in life eternal. Therefore He so often and so decisively contrasts between earthly life and the life of the world to come. Therefore He emphasizes that the latter is the real, the true, the strong, and beautiful life. Every word that He uttered, every one of His acts, every commandment that He gave, every prohibition that He made, all presume life in the hereafter.

B. It was from our Lord's teachings that St. Paul was able to describe the resurrection so magnificently.

1) He says: "In a moment, in the twinkling of an eye, at the last trumpet: for the trumpet shall sound and the dead shall rise again incorruptible, and we shall be changed. For this corruptible must put on incorruption; and this mortal must put on immortality. And when this mortal hath put on immortality, then shall come to pass the saying that is written: Death is swallowed up in victory. O death, where is thy victory? O death, where is thy sting?" (I Cor. 15: 52–55.)

The dead sleep in the earth, as the earth itself sleeps in winter; but they both await the spring.

The dead are motionless in the coffin, just as the chrysalis is motionless in the cocoon, but they await the colorful life of the butterfly.

The dead molder in the grave just as the seed molders in the earth: but both await the renewal of life in spring.

2) We shall also arise, just as Christ arose from death. Christ's soul again united with His body. But what became of that tormented, slain body? The body glorified in resurrection is no longer subject to the laws of matter. It passes through the window like a sunbeam and does not break it. It appears in a room, without the door opening to admit it. It comes and goes among us, the Apostles see it now in one place, then in another. It ascends into the heavens and has no need of elevating forces. Then I shall be like that after my resurrection. Glistening and beautiful and radiant and subject no longer to pain, knowing no limitations of space and time. But that my soul may once gain such a final and perfect

triumph over my body, I must do everything now in earthly life to insure a glorious resurrection.

Do we rise again? Yes. We shall all rise, but not all of us shall rise to life everlasting. Only those rise again to life eternal who, properly speaking, never ceased to live. This is so in all nature. In spring the grass grows again because its roots in the earth were living even in winter's great graveyard. The leaf of a tree shoots forth anew because it lived in the bud. And that man grows and rises again whose soul lived a life of faith and morality. Those who live in sin, who have died in their lifetime, how shall they live after death?

Yes, this is the Christian conception of life everlasting that we gain from our Lord's teaching.

II

THE IDEA OF GOD

If, however, we reflect upon the idea of God in our Christian faith, besides our Lord's clear doctrine we find many other arguments that prove the reality of life hereafter. If God exists, there must also be life hereafter, for such a life is demanded by God's sublimity, His goodness, and His justice.

A. Life continuing after death is demanded by God's sublimity.

1) Only life hereafter and the judgment rendered then will justify God in everything. Here on earth sinners are so audacious, they tread God's laws underfoot with such provocative daring, that the good and the honorable often cry out: "Lord, canst Thou overlook even this? Wilt Thou not punish this either?" Then there must be another life where the sublimity of the offended God receives satisfaction and

where everyone will discover that no one rebels against God with impunity.

2) The wisdom of divine Providence ordering everything for the best, will here be seen. In the confused and painful happenings of this earthly life we have difficulty in perceiving the guiding finger of Providence. Many rebel against God's plans and commands because in world events they see such terrible confusion, just as when one looks at the reverse side of a large Persian rug. So there must be another life, another place, where we see not the reverse side of history's gigantic carpet as has been the case in this earthly life, but its surface. With humble homage we shall then perceive the sublime plans of divine Providence that orders all things for the best and always for our good.

Either there is no sublime God or there is a life everlasting.

B. Life beyond the grave is likewise demanded by God's goodness. There is no life hereafter? Then God is not our benign Father. Could He have created man only to make him miserable?

1) How much man suffers! More than any other living thing in the world. Man knows his sorrow beforehand, he expects it and thus increases it. Then he bemoans it and tears open his wound. Other creatures die, but they know nothing of it beforehand; man knows beforehand and shudders at it. And what is still more dreadful, we have spiritual sufferings: anxiety, grief, when others whom we love have to suffer or die and we are unable to help them.

Man suffers; yet he was not created for suffering, but for happiness. He seeks happiness and longs for it, but in vain: the happiness that he finds in life makes him only more eager. He seeks beauty, but sees that destruction overtakes it; he seeks wealth, well-being, honor, glory: all in vain.

2) If, therefore, I believe in God, I must also believe in life

everlasting. Because God has implanted in me the desire that cannot be gratified here, and that continually cries within me: "To live. To live. And not to die." How the longing for perfect happiness burns within us! And no one finds it in this life. How we strive for perfect light of sight! And no one finds it in this life. We long for peace; and there is no peace. For rest; and there is no rest. For answers to so many questions; and there is no answer. For truth; and there is no truth. How many plans we make; and nothing comes of them. How many things we hope for; and none of our hopes are realized.

My Lord, is it for this Thou hast created man? That he should eat out his heart? Whatever other creature I consider, I see that its desires and the means of attaining them are in proportion the one to the other. An animal satisfies its hunger and is content. But I? I thirst, and earth has no draught that can satisfy my thirst. I need life, I need perfect Beauty, absolute Truth, undisturbed Happiness. And if no such things are attainable? No undisturbed happiness, no life everlasting? Then why hast Thou implanted these desires in me? If truly I was born only to die, then why do I shudder at the thought of dying? Lord, if I may never see Thee, why hast Thou allowed me to know Thee? Why hast Thou created such a void in my heart, that nothing in the world can fill it except Thou thyself, great God?

But I believe that God has not planted deceptive longings in my soul. I believe that, although through thorny paths of suffering, He leads me to eternal life, for God is infinitely good. Either there is no good God, or there is life everlasting.

C. Life hereafter is demanded by God's justice. This belief gives moral world-order its value.

1) How interesting it is to travel on one of the great express trains crossing the continent! What a variety of passengers is

to be seen! A stout merchant is in one of the seats, a thick gold watch-chain adorning his vest; he has a fragrant cigar in his mouth, in his hands is a notorious illustrated paper, and he laughs boisterously as he looks at the pictures. Beside him a priest softly murmurs his breviary: "Gloria Patri et Filio et Spiritui Sancto." A third passenger, a society woman traveling to a pleasure resort, lays aside her novel every half-hour, takes out her mirror and rouges and powders her face. Opposite to her sits a pretty young mother with her two children; she is full of gentleness, full of love. And the train rushes on, rushes on without stopping.

These all arrive at their destination. But those with whom the train of life is rushing on, we human beings squeezed side by side on earth, I wonder if we all reach the same goal. Do we come to the moldering grave, however we have lived on this earth? Then God would not be just. If with death everything is at an end, where do those receive their reward who here on earth endured in honor and in virtue at the price of immense sacrifice? If with death everything is at an end, where do those receive their punishment whom in earthly life the world knew as good and respectable, who were praised and exalted, but in reality their whole lives were full of secret sin and wickedness?

2) O yes. There must be another life where every sin receives its punishment. Here on earth sin often triumphs and gains the victory. But from the lips of embittered and aggrieved individuals we hear this consolation: "Every sin avenges itself. Only wait. A just God will repay."

Is it not this belief that consoles us for all the injustice we have to suffer?

"A just God will repay." Long ago we often heard this said, but perhaps there was never so much to be paid for on earth as today. At other times honesty and sin also strove

together; but immorality never flaunted itself with such cyni-
cal arrogance, and honesty never vegetated so sadly as in
many manifestations of present-day life.

"A just God will some day repay everything." But where
will He repay if there is no continuation to earthly life? If
the grave envelops the innocent and the sinner, the Godfear-
ing and the blasphemer, the murderer and his victim in the
same way, if the grave is the end of everything, what then?
Can we bear this thought? Must this life not be followed by
another, where every sin receives its punishment?

3) And must not God provide another life, where every
virtue receives its due reward? Here on earth the world judges
unjustly; often the good are humbled and the honest oppressed. They find deep consolation in the thought of God's
future realm, where everything will be measured by a very
different standard.

How many worthy, respectable men are justified in saying
of their earthly lives: I never succeed in anything here. If I
start out upon a journey, I am certain to take the wrong turn.
If I take part in a game, I am certain to lose. My friends are
certain to deceive me. My enemies are certain to attack me.
My wine is certain to be watered. My joy is certain to be
turned to gall. And were I to dip my pen in my fate, with
what black ink I should be able to write!

How many could say that!

How greatly, therefore, God's justice requires that there
should be another world where God, as the Savior says, "will
render to every man according to his works"! (Matt. 16: 27.)

Truly, either there is no just God or there is life everlasting.

As my conscience within me and my consciousness of being and every star in the heavens and every flower in the
meadows proclaim that God is, so God's wisdom, goodness,
and justice proclaim that I have an immortal soul and life

everlasting is. Belief in God and belief in life eternal belong inseparably together.

My dear brethren. In the Campo Santo at Genoa this sublime epitaph of three words can be deciphered on an ancient tombstone: *Occido cum sole* ("I set like the sun"). What a comforting thought: Do not weep hopelessly at my death. Who mourns the setting sun at eventide? We know that next day it will rise again in the splendor of dawn. And I, too, have only gone to the grave in this way. I have gone to rest like the sun, and like the sun I shall rise again.

Now we understand what is lacking in Böcklin's famous picture, "The Isle of the Dead." We understand why this picture has a disturbing, depressing effect upon the beholder, in spite of its artistic value. It is because the drooping branches of the mournful cypresses on it are not raised aloft by consoling faith. Because the lowering black clouds are not irradiated by the rays of life everlasting. Because the yawning mouths of the caverns irretrievably swallow the dead, and the words of Christ's promise do not glow above them.

What words? Those which Christ said for the first time at Lazarus' grave to console Martha mourning for her brother, but which since then resound through the world as a divine solace that strengthens our souls mourning our dear dead or trembling at the thought of our own death. "I am the resurrection and the life: he that believeth in Me, although he be dead, shall live: and everyone that liveth and believeth in Me shall not die forever" (John 11: 25, 26).

Occido cum sole. I go to rest like the sun, and like the sun I too shall rise again.

This I believe, this is my sacred conviction, this is my consolation, this is my guide in life. God grant that this may be the reward that I attain. Amen.

IV

REASONABLENESS OF BELIEF IN LIFE EVERLASTING

THERE is no European country so rich in natural beauty as Switzerland, the land that abounds in mountains, forests, glaciers, brooks. Among these natural beauties a prominent place is taken by the Tamina Gorge, the source and bed of the Tamina River. One can go right up to the source, deep in the interior of an immense mountain. Who could say for how many thousands of years this warm water thundered in the depths of the mountain until it hollowed out that gigantic path for itself? There the little rivulet dashes against the subterranean rocks and some irresistible power draws it downward, out of the mountain. At the opening in the mountainside a spa has been erected, Bad Pfäffers. Rheumatic invalids who can hardly move begin to walk again there. And when the water has forced its way through this, it at last reaches the open, the warm sunshine, and, as if reborn, continues its way toward its mouth, toward the river Rhine.

So it is with human life. Through long decades we live here on earth; we dash and bruise ourselves against its stones and rocks and hollow a path for ourselves through the mountain. Some irresistible power draws us constantly nearer to the opening, where death's mysterious spa awaits us. Here we cast off all earthly heaviness, lay aside material life's every support, and soar with fresh impulse in the sunshine of eternal light on the pinions of eternity toward the eternal God.

The German language expresses this clearly when it says that death is not an *Untergang* but an *Ubergang,* not destruction but a crossing over; it is not more than when, going from one room into another, we step across the threshold. Death is the crossing of a threshold.

This belief, the belief in a future life, has always been the common property of mankind. It is plainly proclaimed by our blessed Lord, as well as by the idea of God. To establish this truth by sheer logical reasoning is the task that awaits us in today's sermon.

Today we shall examine those arguments that prove to the philosophical man what the races always believed and what Christianity plainly teaches: there is an immortal soul, there is life everlasting.

The arguments may be divided into three groups: That there is a life hereafter, an immortal soul, is proved by man's mind, by his will, and by his heart.

I

THE TESTIMONY OF REASON

A. Our lives have an object only if there is life everlasting.

1) Everything in the world has some object. That is why a little child asks continually: Why? Why is this so, papa? Why is this so, mamma? But do not tell him that it is for no reason. Because then he will ask: "But if it is for no reason, then why is it at all?"

St. Francis of Assisi once asked a stone-mason:

"What are you doing, brother?"

The man replied: "I am working all day."

"And why are you working?"

"In order to earn money."

"And what do you need money for?"

"That I may have bread."

"And why do you want to have bread?"

"Ha! that is interesting. That I may live."

"And why do you live?"

Yes, this is the great question, the final question: Why do I live? What is the object of my life? Everything in the world has an object. Could only man have none? In me every muscle, nerve, vein, sinew, molecule has its important object. Could only the whole have none? So I must have some object, must I not? Then what is my object?

2) If there is no world to come, my object is evidently here on earth. But what is this object? What is the purpose of my life?

Perhaps to gain wealth? Now is that a worthy object for a clever man? Why, however much I earned, I must leave everything to my heirs, "the laughing heirs," as one often hears them called. And can everyone be wealthy? No indeed. Then why have those lived who could not become rich? Those who have attained their object are at peace; but have those who are wealthy no more desires? Ah, nonsense. They are never at peace. Certainly wealth cannot be the purpose of life.

Then perhaps it is pleasure and enjoyment? No, it cannot be these, because then the greater number of men would never attain their object, so little enjoyment and pleasure is vouchsafed them. And the nearer a being comes to his object the more perfect does he become; but does man become more perfect the more pleasures he enjoys? On the contrary: he becomes so much the more dissatisfied, ill-humored, disspirited.

Then what is man's object? Perhaps to acquire honor and a great name for himself?

O yes, this would be a finer thought than the preceding ones, but it is still not sufficient. How would all those nameless millions attain their object, who, unknown and unsung, quietly do their duty all their lives?

But then what is the object of life? To struggle for sixty, seventy, eighty years and then to disappear, leaving no trace? Can man's reason accept and submit to this? I cast a stone into the water: rings are formed, then everything becomes calm and the water is smooth again. If the stone is a large one, the ripples last for a longer time, but then it also becomes smooth. Can you bear the thought that human life is nothing more than this?

When man, thus tormented, seeks the purpose of life, but finds it nowhere on earth, he raises his eyes beyond earthly things and at once everything becomes clear to him. It is natural that I do not find my purpose on earth. Why? Because God did not create me for this world. This earthly life is but a preface to the book of eternity. In death the body disintegrates, the outer covering falls off; and the undying, eternally living soul remains.

B. But is this possible? Is it possible that we live even after the death of the body?

Christianity's great philosopher and scholar, St. Augustine, relates a Carthaginian doctor's remarkable dream. Genadius —this was the doctor's name—had doubts as to how man could continue to live after the death of the body. In a dream, a radiant youth appeared to him and said:

"Genadius, are you now asleep or awake?"

"I am asleep," replied the doctor.

"Do you see me?" inquired the youth.

"Yes, I see you."

"With what do you see? With your bodily eyes?"

"No, not with them, they are closed. I do not know with what I see you."

But the youth continued to question him: "Genadius, do you hear me?"

"Yes."

"With what do you hear? With your ears?"

"No, not with them. I do not know with what I hear."

And again the youth asked. "Genadius, are you now speaking to me?"

"Yes, I am."

"With what do you speak? With your lips?"

"No, not with them, I do not know with what I speak."

"Now you see," said the angel, "your senses are at rest, yet you see, hear, and speak. And when the hour comes that your senses will rest forever, that is, when you die, then too you will continue to see, to hear, to speak, and to feel."

C. Continuing this thought, we perceive that a new form of life awaits not only our souls in the hereafter, but that not even our bodies are finally destroyed; they too will rise again. The body dies, it is true, but it does not remain dust forever.

1) Were it to remain dust, then the Almighty's most beautiful thought would remain incomplete. Is the human body not worthy to be raised from death by the Creator? Among all created material things, the human body is the Creator's most beautiful work. The May sunshine is glorious; but can it be so radiant as the tender smile of a human being? Dawn in spring is beautiful; but is not the angelic glance of a pure-souled youth more beautiful? The starry sky enchants us; but what is it compared to the clear eyes of a child? Birds trill delightfully; but what is that compared to the voice of man? How beautiful man must have been when he left his Maker's hands and still radiated his likeness to God, how beautiful he must have been, if even now, defiled by sin, he so greatly surpasses everything around him!

2) Now tell me: is it credible that God allows this work of His to be annihilated for all time? The stars have been shining for thousands of years, and their brilliance has not expired. How many thousand springtimes the earth has already seen, and its fertility is not exhausted. Wells bubble, valleys blossom, mountains tower aloft, everything lives on. Can only man's fate be a few brief years and then the grave, silence, and a crumbling to dust?

Should even man's own works outlive him? Here around us stand the old houses of this city. They were built, some of them, a hundred years ago, and still stand. But where are their builders? In our public squares we see statues that were made decades ago. They stand, and those who carved them died long ago. But are those sculptors annihilated? A man paints his own portrait. Does this copy live longer than the original, who was created by almighty God Himself? No. I cannot believe this.

3) Rather do I think, if I may use a comparison, that as the insect creeping in the dust winds itself into its cocoon, enclosing itself in a motionless tomb, afterward to emerge with new strength in a beautiful new body, and the gaudy butterfly then no longer descends to the dust, but alights only on flowers, so the heavy, awkward, sick body made of dust first descends to the grave, but afterward loses all heaviness, and when it rises it is noble, spiritual, it can no longer suffer, and it is more radiant than the stars of heaven.

Yes, there is a great difference between the man moldering in the grave and the man who lives eternally. But is there not a great difference between the chrysalis lying motionless in its cocoon and the gaily colored butterfly? Yet the butterfly was once a motionless chrysalis.

"There will be no resurrection because we cannot understand how the next life would be," say doubters. But do you understand how this first life came to be? Who understands this? And if God was able to give life that had not been, can He not give back that which had once already been?

Truly, the reality of life everlasting is proved by man's reasoning mind. But it is also proved by man's will.

II

THE TESTIMONY OF MAN'S WILL

A. With an elemental urge we long for justice. This is so deeply rooted in our natures that even a four-year-old child becomes sad, without knowing why, when it hears of the unjust suffering that Cinderella had to endure from her wicked stepmother.

1) But where is justice to be found on this earth? On all sides we see honor trampled upon and evil triumphant. Yet we cannot bear the thought that evil triumphs over good. Earthly life is filled with discord, but we feel that somewhere things will be equalized. No dramatist would venture to end his play with the triumph of evil. The spectators would say, and rightly: "The play is not finished." In modern music there is dissonance, but at last every dissonance must dissolve into harmony.

2) But life must not end with the triumph of sin. Can deception triumph? Can wickedness triumph? Can evil triumph? Can he who tramples God's laws underfoot triumph? Yet if there is no hereafter, the wicked triumph. If there is no hereafter, then however people have spent their lives, their fate is the same: to molder in the grave. But who can bear this thought?

A sister of mercy is dying. Her whole life has been an unceasing sacrifice of love toward her fellow men. Now she is dying of the typhoid fever contracted while nursing typhoid patients. And an old voluptuary is dying too, who has wallowed in sin all his life and is now dying impenitent after the most dreadful dissipation. Can the same fate await both of them? Can anyone in sober sense bear this thought?

B. The longing for eternal life is so deeply rooted in men's souls that not even the foes of Christianity can free themselves from it. History abounds with examples of how the defiant voice of the atheists is stilled in moments of mortal danger.

When cholera raged in France in the year 1835, even the so-called "enlightened" freethinkers walked barefoot in the streets of Paris with lighted candles in their hands, beating their breasts and praying: *Parce, Domine!* ("Have mercy, Lord!").

And did not the monster of the French Revolution, Camille Desmoulins, write to his wife before being led to execution: "Not concerned with my torments, I believe that God exists. Lucille, we shall meet again."

III

THE TESTIMONY OF MAN'S HEART

What we conclude from the functions of mind and will by mere human reasoning—life everlasting beyond the grave—must also be inferred from the different manifestations of the human heart.

A. The human heart yearns with elemental force for happiness. We are thus created: we long to be happy. Do you not hear the unceasing cry of millions for happiness? Do you not see the restless striving of millions to attain happiness?

1) But where on this earth is happiness? Where can you find complete, imperishable, undisturbed happiness? Man seeks happiness, turning night into day with self-sacrificing work, as the ancients sought "the philosopher's stone"; and

man does not succeed in finding it, just as they did not succeed.

We need complete happiness. Give every earthly treasure to man; for a day he is happy, but then he asks: "Is that all?" Even Alexander the Great, at the very zenith of his triumphs, began to weep as he said: "There are still the stars. Those I cannot add to my conquests."

And we need imperishable happiness. The happier man is, the more dreadful is the thought: This is transient, everything is transient.

2) If there is no hereafter, God is but playing with us. He has planted a desire in us, the desire for happiness, which we can never attain. Why has God given us this consuming longing for perfect justice, for imperishable happiness, if this longing is never to be gratified?

If the natives of mountainous districts come to the plains, they feel a homesickness for the snowy heights where they were born. Thus, too, our souls respond to all that is beautiful, good, and true, because their true home is another realm where perfect Beauty, Goodness, and Truth are enthroned.

3) "With death everything is at an end. Life is at an end, all happiness is at an end." These words are easily said. But try to believe it when you stand at the deathbed of your beloved wife or your precious child. Try to believe it at the funeral of your mother.

Maternal love. There is no word on earth that rings more warmly, no more trustworthy, blessed loyalty. Never, never could I believe that when her dear earthly remains were lowered into the grave, I lost my mother forever. Lost the love with which she nursed me in my infancy, which accompanied me when I became a grown man? Lost forever? No. This I will never believe.

B. But man longs not only for happiness, but also for justice. Since the first man gazed up questioningly, searchingly at the stars, an unappeasable thirst for truth beset the human race.

1) But how much truth do we find on this earth? What tiny grains of it! What fragments of it! What is it then in us that thirsts so longingly for complete truth? Where shall we find this, if not in that realm which Newman refers to in his epitaph: *Ex umbris et imaginibus in veritatem* ("From shadows and symbols he passed to the realm of truth").

Man always feels his imperfection, always seeks something better, something greater. We are travelers; somewhere a destination awaits us.

Man seeks life. But we possess life. Ah, nonsense! What we possess here on earth is only a tiny crumb of life, only a shadow of life. A bud not yet unfolded. A drop of nectar for whose source we yearn.

2) Human life here on earth is never consummated, we never finish with ourselves. Therefore there must be another life, a life of consummation, of perfection. How affecting is the confession of that genius, Michelangelo who, after ninety years spent in creating the most beautiful works of art, said two days before his death: "I regret only two things: that I did not care more for the salvation of my soul and that I must die just when I am beginning to stammer the first words of my art."

Or there are Victor Hugo's words: "I draw nearer and nearer to my end and hear around me ever more clearly the deathless symphony of the worlds that call to me. It is such a wonderful and simple thing! For half a century I have written down my thoughts in prose and poem. I have tried everything, but I feel that I have not said a thousandth part of what lives within me."

You know perhaps the legend of the mother whose son was deaf and dumb. The boy died without having been able even once to speak his mother's name. The woman lived for many long years, silently bearing the grief in her aching heart. She became old and died. And see, at the gates of heaven her son met her with the joyful cry of: "Mother! My own dear Mother!"

Always, with instinctive certainty, mankind has felt that there must be a place where our noblest desires are realized, the desires that dwell within us but are never realized here on earth.

3) But is this eternal longing within us only vain imagining? Does this instinctive feeling of ours delude us?

With the first cold autumn wind, the swallows become restless. An irresistible instinct drives them toward the south where they find warm nests and a certainty of food, when here with us the chill of winter covers the earth and the insects hide away. The little swallow hatched here this season, which has never yet seen a winter, goes too. The swallow hatched in a cage that has never had to seek its food, becomes restless and, if we free it, it goes away too. Whither do they fly? Far away, to a southern world, that they have never seen, that they have never heard of. What takes them? Natural science says they are impelled by instinct.

Well and good. Nature has given them this instinct. And if they were deceived? If no warmth awaited them down south, but icy cold and death? Would this instinct have any meaning? No. Nature would have deceived them. But nature is not in the habit of deceiving her creatures. If the swallow could think, it would say: "It is quite certain that there is another world, for my instinct says there is."

The swallow cannot think. However, I can and I say:

"There must be a hereafter, because my reason, my will, and my heart all say that this life has a continuation, a consummation; there is life everlasting."

My dear brethren. Deep thinkers feel as though they were walking in shadow here on earth: everything is only a beginning, everything is half-accomplished work, always some dissatisfaction drives them. They feel that there should be a place where the sunshine is perfect and where the song that we sing will be perfect, as in the story of the violinist.

There once lived a violinist who determined to learn to play the most beautiful melody to be found on earth. He often went to the forest to hear the song of birds. Then of a sudden he was able to play so charmingly that people thought they heard the lark and the nightingale singing. It was beautiful, but for our violinist it was not beautiful enough.

So he sought the soft zephyr and listened to its tender melody. He stood in the raging storm and listened to its wild roaring. And he learned this too. His violin sang like a softly murmuring breeze among the leaves, then thundered like the storm that bends great oaks at its will. It was sublime: but for our violinist it was not yet beautiful enough.

Then he observed the waters and with his violin he imitated the frenzy of mountain torrents, the thundering of the surf, the rippling murmur of some purling little brook. It was beautiful; but our violinist was still dissatisfied.

Then he went among men. He played all the joyous songs of youth, lively dances, and mournful melodies; he played religious tunes too. Now and again his heart beat quicker at an air welling up from the depths of the human soul. But the most beautiful song, the song that he had restlessly longed for all his life, he still could not find.

Meanwhile he had become gray, old, and sick unto death. As he lay awaiting his last hour, see, suddenly from a great distance wonderful music fell upon his ear. That is it! That is the song he sought all his life: the most beautiful, the most sublime song. Gathering together the last remnants of his strength, he seizes his violin, his hand shakes, his fingers tremble, yet he plays the song, the most beautiful song sought for and presaged all his life. And as he ended the last note of the song, all four strings of his violin snapped, and he fell back on his pillows—dead.

He found the most beautiful song in God's eternal kingdom. Amen.

V

THE FRUIT OF BELIEF IN LIFE EVERLASTING

In grape-growing districts a strange thing is spoken of by the vinedressers. They say that in spring, when the force of new life rises in the branches and the vines begin to sprout, the wine in the depths of the cellars becomes disturbed, fomenting and seething in the casks as if some mysterious connection existed between it and the vine from which it came; it is as though the wine rejoiced that new life is sprouting in the vine on which its grapes once grew.

Perhaps the whole thing is only imagination. No imagination, however, but sacred fact is the truth that, as often as our souls turn in thought to the eternal home where they will some day return, a restless holy joy fills us. We feel the urge and encouragement that earthly life receives from the thought of life everlasting.

Of course I am thinking of those who are consistent to their principles, whose whole manner of life shows that they believe in eternal life. Because, regrettably enough, some who accept this theoretically and even avow belief in life everlasting, do not accept it in their hearts. We see just as little of it in their lives as in the lives of those who are altogether unbelieving.

We sometimes say that a certain matter "must be taken to heart." By this expression we mean not only that a truth must be believed and understood by the mind, but that it must also be accepted in the heart, that is, we must accept it so that it permeates our entire being and directs our thoughts, our feelings, and our wills. Today I wish to bring the truth of life everlasting to your hearts and point out that belief in life everlasting gives an impulse to life, strength in temptation, and courage in suffering.

I

SPIRITUAL POWER

The earthly existence of a person who does not believe in life everlasting may be compared to a bridge that has collapsed part way across the river and does not reach the opposite bank. On the other hand, a believer gains wings with this belief, wings that enable him to rise to heights unattainable by unbelievers. A certain sociologist says that belief in the immortality of the soul is "the greatest cultural factor in all history" because this belief gives a purpose to man's life and thus completely transforms his life.

A. Christianity's importance and value, its sublime impulse, its splendid activity, spring from the belief in life everlasting. This is the goal that we must attain.

1) Those who do not live the religious life of an earnest believer have no idea what a source of spiritual endeavor is derived from belief in life everlasting. Believers fervently pray for this and strive for it. With this end in view, they practice much self-denial and perform many good deeds.

This is the reason for the sacraments and various devotional practices, for sacrifice and renunciation, fasting and self-discipline, churches, reason for the unceasing conflict with our sinful natures. This is the reason for the serious acceptance of our Lord's words: "Strive to enter by the narrow gate, for many, I say to you, shall seek to enter, and shall not be able" (Luke 13: 24).

2) We sometimes hear the reproach that Christianity lowers the value of earthly life because it always speaks of the life hereafter, of the world to come. The very opposite is true: belief in life everlasting increases the value of earthly life.

Since eternal life depends wholly on a well spent earthly life, the value of earthly life grows to gigantic proportions. From belief in life eternal springs our love of work. This is apparently a contradiction. Yet the wearing, monotonous work of everyday life, upon which all human culture has been erected and on which it depends, can be accomplished only by a humanity on whom its belief has impressed a sense of duty, a feeling that, by fidelity to the tasks of earthly life, life everlasting is to be gained.

3) Again, only belief in life everlasting keeps the instinctive desire for earthly work and earthly wealth within rightful bounds. Whoever does not believe in the continuation of earthly life naturally scrapes together money and treasures with all his ten fingers, not allowing another to enjoy anything of his possessions, trampling upon everyone in this pursuit of greed. Whereas he in whom belief in life everlasting is a guiding principle regards earthly life as something transient and does not concentrate all his desires and labors on such fleeting things.

Whatever the world gives to such a man, it is not enough for him. He wants eternal happiness, eternal life. His ideal is St. Philip Neri who, when told that the pope intended to make him a cardinal, threw his hat into the air and cried out: "Paradise is what I want, not the purple."

For such a man, the sort of "eternal" life proclaimed by unbelief is not sufficient: "Your atoms will circulate eternally in the cosmic void because nothing is ever lost"; "your thoughts continue to work"; "you will be honored by a splendid statue." This is not sufficient for me. If I am dead, do not write my biography in dead letters, on dead paper; do not carve any statue of me that a facsimile of my figure may stand in dead stone or cold bronze silently and blindly by the wayside. I need life after death, real life, life everlasting. He who created me for earthly life, shall now give me new life, but more beautiful, happier, life that never ends. This is the stupendous goal before which belief in life everlasting places me.

B. In placing this exalted end before us, Christianity transforms our whole earthly life.

1) On one occasion the Greek philosopher Zeno asked the oracle what he must do to live a virtuous life. The answer was merely these few words: "Ask the dead."

Those who are accustomed to ask the dead—which in Christian language means that they are in the habit of thinking of the next life—will view earthly life and all its happenings in quite another light. *Sub specie aeternitatis* ("from the viewpoint of eternity"); they will weigh everything against the thought of eternal life, their every project, thought, desire, will be imbued with the breath of eternity, ennobling and refining them.

In life they will strive to keep God's laws and the laws of the Church, because they know that everything—attendance at mass, the use of the sacraments, prayer, fasting, self-discipline—all serve this eternal life.

They also work hard for a livelihood, for advancement in their earthly career, but in every endeavor the Lord's words are before them: "What doth it profit a man if he gain the whole world and suffer the loss of his own soul?" (Matt. 16: 26.)

They also try to secure a respectable livelihood. But in face of temptation to acquire wealth by unjust means, they remember the Lord's words: "Thou fool. This night do they require thy soul of thee, and whose shall those things be which thou hast provided?" (Luke 12: 20.)

In a word, those who seriously consider life everlasting, who not only believe in it but also take it to heart, will judge earthly life from the standpoint of eternity and will live it accordingly. They will stand firmly on the earth, because they must live here; but their hearts will beat heavenward, their heads will be uplifted to the stars.

2) Some wonder whether life everlasting is worth so much toil, so much self-denial.

A thousand times more. For what is life everlasting? We use phrases whose meaning we never fully grasp. *Per omnia saecula saeculorum,* we pray. But no one can fully understand what this means. Here on earth we are enclosed in space, time, matter, but the next life has no space, no time, no matter, there time is not composed of minutes and hours. There is no past and future, only present. There is no yesterday and tomorrow, only today. There is no morning and evening, only noon. There the ocean has no shore, there a line has no end. That is, we cannot measure eternity with a line, but rather with a circle, because a line, however much prolonged, has an end somewhere, but a circle has no end anywhere, every part of it is both the beginning and the end.

Here the truth of St. Augustine's words becomes evident: "Ye poor, what do you lack if you possess God? Ye rich, what do you possess if you lack God?"

Here we understand Gardonyi's words: "If you possess God, you possess everything; but if you have no God, you do not possess anything and never will possess anything."

II

BELIEF IN LIFE EVERLASTING GIVES STRENGTH IN
TEMPTATION

Belief in life everlasting not only marks an exalted goal for earthly life; it is also strength against temptations that would keep us from our eternal goal.

A. Our Lord so often mentions the serious thought of life everlasting in order to make us capable of sacrifice.

1) *Sacrifice everything to gain life everlasting.* This is Christ's doctrine and exhortation. Yes, even if one of your hands or one of your eyes is lost in the struggle. Starvation and prison, suffering and martyrdom in this world do not count, if you gain the world to come. This voice cries from the cross: You fight a life and death struggle: here you must not fall.

That this life everlasting is no lottery prize that falls unexpectedly into our hands, but must be won by contending heroically all our lives, is a matter of course. "Fight the good fight of faith, lay hold on eternal life; keep the commandment without spot" (I Tim. 6: 12, 14), writes St. Paul to Timothy.

2) Keep the commandment, for to be good is so beautiful and tranquillizing. Sometimes this reasoning is sufficient. But, alas, sometimes temptation assails us so mightily that nothing helps us to withstand it except the belief in life everlasting, the fear that we may spoil forever our lives hereafter.

A father was loudly disputing with some friends, saying that he did not believe in heaven and in hell. His wife, pointing to their little girl playing in a corner of the room, whispered:

"Do not talk like that before the child."

The father waved her aside: "She does not understand

what I am talking about." Then he turned to the child saying: "Do you understand what papa is saying?"

The child's eyes shone triumphantly as she said proudly: "Yes."

"Well, what did I say?"

"That nobody needs to be good."

How right the child was! What restrains, if anything at all restrains our youth from dissipation, from dishonorable deeds, except the thought of life everlasting? And those who sin and begin to slip downhill, what do they forsake first? Belief in life everlasting. What gives a person strength to perform his duty when others neglect theirs? What gives strength for the struggle to preserve our moral integrity in poverty, when by merely closing our eyes to one or two little things we might achieve success at once in this world? What gives strength for honest work when we might go farther with deception? Belief in life everlasting.

B. Life everlasting is a powerful warning in times of temptation.

1) When St. Paul was a prisoner in Caesarea, the Roman governor Felix brought the Apostle before him to question him. All the power of the Roman Empire was behind Felix. Before him stood the prisoner in chains, between armed soldiers. Yet Holy Writ notes that when St. Paul began to preach to him of justice and chastity and of the judgment to come, Felix was terrified (Acts 24: 25). Belief in a life beyond the grave, the thought of a reckoning to be made, may well terrify not only the Roman governor, but everyone else.

2) If only we were to think of this often! Especially when alluring temptations assail us.

A certain chief of police in Paris had an interesting method in his campaign against the noise made in the streets by intoxicated persons. He simply had a film made of them, and

showed it to them when they had become sober. The effect
was amazing. In a sober state they were utterly ashamed of the
foolish actions and coarse language they had used while intoxicated.

An immense film runs round the world, God's all-embrac-
ing knowledge. On this film appear our every word, every
deed, every desire, every plan, every secret. Alas, what a dis-
grace it will be when this film is produced on judgment day,
when by the glow of eternal light we shall see in our sober
senses what we foolishly committed in the intoxication of
earthly life!

3) I am sorry to say that people do not like to think of this.
They are engrossed by earthly cares. On the day of judgment
they will fare as a famous historian fared who was exploring
the country of the Nile. While crossing the river, he began
talking to the boatman.

"Are you acquainted with the Sanscrit language?" he asked.

"No, sir," answered the boatman.

"Can you recognize the stars?"

"No, sir."

"Do you know anything of the history of this earth?"

"I do not, sir."

"Man!" cried the scholar; "you have lost half your life."

Suddenly a great storm of wind arose, and the boisterous
waves upset the boat.

"Sir," shouted the boatman; "do you know how to swim?"

"I do not."

"Then you have lost your whole life, sir."

The boatman reached the shore with difficulty, but the
scholar was drowned.

Many people are interested in various things here on earth,
in many things, but not in life everlasting. Many superfluous
things they acquire in their lives, but they do not see to it that

they know how to swim when the storm of the last judgment breaks.

III

BELIEF IN LIFE EVERLASTING IS ENCOURAGEMENT IN SUFFERING

Belief in life everlasting gives us courage in suffering. However human life is perfected here on earth, suffering will always be the lot of man: calamities of nature, privation, illness, pain, and there will always be death.

If the grave is the last act in life, then life is a great tragedy. But what suffering, catastrophe, disaster, affliction I can bear if I believe in life everlasting!

A. "I believe in life everlasting." What a source of strength this belief is in the struggle of life! What endurance in suffering! Have you ever noticed the blind? Their faces are always turned upward. If this world is dark about me, the next world gives me light.

In time of suffering the greatest men have derived strength from their belief in life everlasting. Thus it was with those two luminaries of human genius, St. Augustine and Dante, when their souls were assailed by gnawing pangs of suffering. Do you know what strengthened these two stupendous intellects for battle? Flaming love for the eternal home, the fiery vision of life everlasting, the power of the thought of life hereafter that superseded every other thought and desire.

So it was with Sir Thomas More, the great English chancellor, when he refused to approve the divorce of Henry VIII and consequently was deprived of his high office and was sent to the Tower. Neither promise nor threat could shake him. Finally his wife and weeping children visited him in prison. Throwing herself on her knees. his wife implored him:

"Think how long we could live happily together. Why will you die so young?"

"How long might we expect to live?" More asked.

"For twenty years at least," replied his wife.

"Twenty years. For the sake of twenty years shall I give up my eternal life, my eternal happiness?"

And after seventeen months of imprisonment, he courageously laid his head upon the executioner's block on July 6, 1535.

Belief in life everlasting gives courage in suffering.

B. But only if this belief is truly living in me. The inspired word says: "Remember thy Creator in the days of thy youth before the time of affliction come . . . and the dust return into its earth from whence it was, and the spirit return to God who gave it" (Eccles. 12: 1, 7).

St. Paul says: "We have not here a lasting city, but we seek one that is to come" (Heb. 13: 14). Brethren, do you believe this?

St. Paul underwent great and many sufferings. Yet he is almost beside himself with joy and can hardly find words in his enthusiasm when he thinks of the resurrection: "One is the glory of the sun, another the glory of the moon, and another the glory of the stars. For star differeth from star in glory. So also is the resurrection of the dead. It is sown in corruption, it shall rise in incorruption. It is sown in dishonor, it shall rise in glory. It is sown in weakness, it shall rise in power. It is sown a natural body, it shall rise a spiritual body" (I Cor. 15: 41–44).

Tell me, do you believe this? In the midst of suffering can you comfort yourself with such joyful certainty as St. Paul comforted himself with? "We faint not. . . . For that which is at present momentary and light of our tribulation, worketh for us above measure exceedingly an eternal weight of glory"

(II Cor. 4: 16, 17). "For we know, if our earthly house of this habitation be dissolved, that we have a building of God, a house not made with hands, eternal in heaven" (II Cor. 5: 1). But tell me, brethren, do you believe this? Do you believe it, not only "perhaps," "eventually," "it may be," "it would be beautiful if it were so"? No. But do you believe it so that your whole life, your every plan and desire, are permeated and directed by this belief?

Newton, the renowned scientist, was once asked this question: "Man's body becomes dust. If the resurrection really takes place, who will collect the millions and millions of dispersed grains of dust to make a new body for the soul?" Newton did not reply. He seized a handful of iron filings, mixed them with sand and then asked: "Who will collect these dispersed filings again?" And when no one could answer him, he seized a magnet and held it above the mixture. At once a stir and motion began in the sand, and the tiny particles of iron flew to the magnet and clung to it. The master then said earnestly: "Can He who gave this power to dead matter not give still greater power to our souls when, from the glorified dust, they will have need of garments?"

This I believe. And this belief of mine is the object of my life, strength in temptation, and encouragement in all suffering.

My dear brethren. You know the splendid courage of Christopher Columbus which enabled him to start out to find a new continent never before seen or discovered by anyone.

Novum desidero mundum, he cried, "I seek a new world." And however much his companions grumbled, however little faith they possessed, whatever difficulties he had to contend with, he persevered. He persevered until he landed at that other shore that he had never seen.

We do not see the next world, at least not with our bodily

eyes. But we see it with the eyes of faith and seize upon it with the power of our mind.

We see it with the eyes of faith. One might say there is no gesture of our Lord that does not point to this world to come. One might say our Lord has no word that does not possess this keynote: Seek, before all else and above all else, at whatever sacrifice, this life hereafter.

And we capture it with the power of our mind. If God exists, there must be life everlasting before His throne. If God indeed exists, there must be a place where every hidden act of goodness receives its reward, but also every sin its punishment. If God exists, there must be a place where the longing that dwells in everyone is satisfied, the longing for perfect happiness and justice.

O blessed belief in life everlasting! To what stupendous heights it exalts us, man smitten to the dust by the thought of perishing! How it animates us! How it consoles us! How it encourages us!

In the preface of the funeral mass we find these beautiful words: "We give thanks to Thee, O holy Lord, Father almighty, everlasting God: through Christ our Lord. In whom the hope of a blessed resurrection hath shone upon us; that those whom the certainty of dying afflicteth, the promise of future immortality may console. For unto Thy faithful, O Lord, life is changed, not taken away: and the abode of this earthly sojourn being dissolved, an eternal dwelling is prepared in heaven."

I await this eternal dwelling place, I await this life everlasting. Life everlasting, where the reward of my faith will be knowledge, the reward of my hope possession, and the reward of my love, of my feeble love, will be the reciprocation and crown of the eternal love of the infinite God. Amen.

VI

THE GATE OF LIFE EVERLASTING: DEATH

"I BELIEVE in the resurrection of the body and life everlasting."
With these triumphant words our Creed ends. From this belief emanates strength, encouragement, and consolation for
us in our spiritual life. Belief in life everlasting gives a purpose to our lives, strength in temptation, and consolation in
suffering. Besides all these blessed fruits produced by our belief in life everlasting, is another fruit, the solution of the
problem of death.

Death is mankind's most torturing problem. However
greatly we have loved another, however firmly we have clung
to another, however closely related we have been, death in-
evitably comes and at the grave speaks to us in hard tones:
"Now you must say farewell: you must part."

Belief in life everlasting, however, consoles us, and it alone
consoles us, in this grief. Belief in life everlasting can give an
answer, and it alone can give an answer, to this most painful
question. Belief in life everlasting solves the problem of
death.

On the face of death I wish to project the light of life everlasting.

I

THE GATE OF LIFE EVERLASTING IS DEATH

A. Everyone must pass through the gate of death.

1) Ezechias, the king of the Jews, lay seriously ill when

Isaias went to him and told him the Lord's message: "Thus
saith the Lord God: Give charge concerning thy house, for
thou shalt die and not live" (IV Kings, 20: 1).

"Thou shalt die." When these words fell from the prophet's
lips, the king's soul shuddered. He turned his face to the wall
and began to pray: "I beseech Thee, O Lord, remember how
I have walked before Thee in truth and with a perfect heart
and have done that which is pleasing before Thee (IV Kings,
20: 3). Thus the terrified king prayed and broke into bitter
weeping.

"Thou shalt die," were the prophet's words. Who among
us would not start weeping if he heard this? "Die? No. I do
not want to die. I want to live." Would we not all say this?

2) Yes, man wants to live. Even in ancient times men tried
their best to overcome disease. And when death triumphed
after all, at least they built pyramids as sepulchers, marble
tombstones, memorials, obelisks, epitaphs. But men longed
to live; yet they died.

An Arabian proverb says: "If the house is finished one
must die." So the Arab never completely finishes his house,
yet he dies.

In Chicago, a convention of undertakers decided not to
paint coffins black any more, but rather all the colors of the
rainbow, in order to soften the depressing effect of funerals;
yet people die there, too.

Once upon a time it was said that all roads lead to Rome.
Yet in very truth we can rightly say that all roads lead to
death. Nothing else is so certain as death. In German, if you
wish to declare that something is quite certain, you say, *Tod-
sicher,* "as certain as death."

"Vanity of vanities, said Ecclesiastes, vanity of vanities, and
all is vanity. What hath a man more of all his labor that he
taketh under the sun?" (Eccles. 1: 2, 3.) "I have seen all

things that are done under the sun, and behold all is vanity and vexation of spirit" (Eccles. 1: 14). "Whatsoever my eyes desired, I refused them not; and I withheld not my heart from enjoying every pleasure." "And when I turned myself to all the works which my hands had wrought, and of the labors wherein I had labored in vain, I saw in all things vanity, and vexation of mind, and that nothing was lasting under the sun" (Eccles. 2: 10, 11).

Böcklin has painted an instructive picture of "the four ages of life." In the foreground a meadow is seen with a purling brook and two little children playing on its bank. In the center to the right a young woman stands with a bunch of fresh flowers in her hand. To the left a knight with courageous expression starts out upon his steed to battle with life. In the background on a little hill rising above a cave, sits a weary old man with bent back; leaning upon his stick he gazes into the distance: thus he awaits death who approaches unperceived from behind. From the cave a stream of water flows ceaselessly, the symbol of eternally fleeting time, and above the cave this inscription is seen: *Vita somnium breve,* "Life is a brief dream."

It is indeed a brief dream. The psalmist says to God: "A thousand years in Thy sight are as yesterday which is past, and as a watch in the night. Things that are counted nothing, shall their years be. In the morning man shall grow up like grass, in the morning he shall flourish and pass away; in the evening he shall fall, grow dry and wither" (Ps. 89: 4–6).

Life is a brief dream. From every dream one must awake. Death is an awaking from the earthly dream to the reality of life everlasting.

B. Through the gate of death everyone must pass, for "it is appointed unto men once to die" (Heb. 9: 27), says Holy Writ.

1) Gerard Kempis, brother of Thomas, built himself a beautiful palace and invited his friends to come and admire it. Everyone praised the house, only one had some objection to make.

"Your palace is beautiful," he said; "but I should like to give you a piece of advice."

"And what is that?" asked his host.

"Wall up one door."

"Which one?"

"The one through which you will some day be carried to the cemetery."

But this door cannot be walled up.

Death is not merely an unpleasant guest whom we cannot get rid of. He is a member of the family, he belongs in the home, and knows no mercy with either young or old.

The hotels at some Italian health resorts display this proud inscription: *Qui si sana,* "here health is regained." Of course, some invalids do recover their health. But no sanatorium in the world would dare display this declaration: "Here people do not die." Such a sanatorium is not to be found.

2) Who does not shudder when in some cemetery he surveys death's dominion? How much pomp, how much power, how much prosperity and splendor lie buried beneath the silent tombstones, that seem to remind us of Holy Writ's warning: "Vanity of vanities, all is vanity" (Eccles. 1:2).

3) Death is no respecter of persons, he is not biased in anyone's favor. Whom death will take and when, is God's secret, the secret we human beings will never solve.

There are thousands for whom death would be a release, thousands whose death would be a relief for those about them, and they live, live on for many years. Others, who seem to be needed by their family, others who could do so much good, who could labor so much for the Church of God—these must go. Who can understand this? Only he who reads God's words in Holy Writ: "My thoughts are not your thoughts nor your ways My ways" (Is. 55:8). "It is appointed unto men once to die" (Heb. 9:27). Therefore nothing is so certain in life as that we must die.

C. Since this is so, if we think in a serious Christian way we do well to become familiar with the thought and earnestly to prepare our souls for that tremendous hour.

1) The Christian way is often to ask the question: When will death come for me? On which day? In what guise? Slyly, like a thief? Will it fall upon me like a robber? At home? Or at the street corner? I do not know. Therefore I must always be prepared; my soul must be set in order. Death may come at any time.

Every day approximately 120,000 people die, every day 120,000 verdicts are passed. Among these are all kinds of men: counts, dukes, streetcleaners, stonebreakers, gipsies, all come to judgment. Now and again comes a king, a bishop, a pope. But they no longer bear any mark of distinction, there is no crown upon their heads, no papal tiara, no purple on their shoulders, no ermine, no evening clothes, no dinner-jacket; nothing but the snow-white robe of sanctifying grace. This is the Court dress of the heavenly kingdom.

To those who wear this "wedding garment" (Matt. 22:12), no matter what they were in earthly life, the gates of God's kingdom are opened wide. Those who are without it, no matter how many decorations were carried on velvet cushions in their funeral processions, cannot escape the verdict. For we do not take anything with us there, no medals, automobiles, estates, checkbooks, nothing but our own inner values. What we had, we cannot take with us, only what we were. This is the Christian way of growing familiar with death.

2) The Jews of the Old Testament, according to the testi-

mony of Deuteronomy, had to go three times annually to the holy place appointed, and the sacred writer adds the warning: "No one shall appear with his hands empty before the Lord" (Deut. 16: 16). We, too, come before the Lord, but only once, at the time of our death. Let us not appear with empty hands.

Therefore it is a Christian proceeding to think of death and accept the scriptural warning: "O that they would be wise and would understand, and would provide for their last end" (Deut. 32: 29).

Man is a master of self-deception, he can deceive himself in many ways, but never more fatally, never more painfully, than when he postpones repentance until the moment of death. It is almost an impossibility that anyone should be able to put his soul in order when he is enduring the torments of a fatal illness, if, when healthy, he never troubled about his soul at all. It is no wonder that in such cases the words which the Savior once spoke to His enemies are fulfilled: "I go, and you shall seek Me and you shall die in your sin" (John 8: 21).

Dear Lord, let not this threat be fulfilled in me. But rather: "Let my soul die the death of the just, and my last end be like to them" (Num. 23: 10).

II

HOW SHALL WE PASS THROUGH THE GATE OF DEATH?

"It is appointed unto men once to die, and after this the judgment" (Heb. 9: 27). What will dying be like, and what will the judgment afterward be like?

A. What will dying be like?

1) Strictly speaking, earthly life itself is a continuous dying. A continual struggle against illness, against growing old, and against death. We are like a bird perched on a branch. Beneath it the flood increases, and the bird hops to a higher

branch. But when it feels that the topmost branch of the tree will also be flooded and there is no other way of escape, it spreads its wings and flies away. We, too, lengthen our lives in every way as long as possible. But when this is no longer possible, our soul spreads its wings and flies away: this is death.

2) The spiritual fortifying of the dying is one of the Catholic priest's most difficult, yet at the same time, most moving duties. The moment when the torch of earthly life prepares to flicker out is a very affecting one, and I, a priest of Christ, have to summon all my wisdom, all my love, all my strength that the soul may be at its clearest when the moment of passing comes, and may turn wholly to God in its last moments.

When the last tremor has passed through the mortal body, when the heart has throbbed for the last time and death has come, a nameless emotion, grief, distress, takes possession of each of us. Innumerable questions throng our minds: "Your body lies here dead, but what is happening now to your soul? What happened at the moment your soul left your body and appeared before its Judge? And what was the verdict? Where are you now? Immensely far away from us or quite near us? Do you still recognize us? Do you still remember us, your relatives, your friends? Or have you forgotten everyone and everything of this world?"

3) What can the moment of death be like? No one knows. Those who have experienced it can no longer tell us about it.

What is the moment like, when the instinct of preservation would make a final spasmodic clutch at life, but death intervenes. It is as though we had arrived at a dark tunnel; everything grows dim, everything disappears. Have you ever had the unpleasant dream of falling precipitately downward into a dark void? Our hands and feet are bound and we cannot move; we wish to scream, but not a sound escapes our lips, we only fall downward, downward. Will the moment of death be like that? Who can say?

Have you ever been on the operating table in a hospital? An anesthetic is administered. The world begins to disappear. Our heads seem to grow larger; now it is as though we were flying, without wings, far far away into the endless distance. Will the moment of death be like that? Who could say? Only one who has been through it. But he cannot speak to us any more.

B. He does not speak to us because he is standing before the judgment seat of God, and now comes God's verdict.

1) At the moment of death the world to come is disclosed to the soul. But what will this first glimpse of the immeasurable realm of infinite light be like? Perhaps it will be like the falling of a rose into the sea when its white petals are embraced on all sides and rocked by the murmuring waves. Shall I perhaps in this way be permeated and transformed to dazzling brilliance amid the billowing ocean of light?

This is the "perpetual light" that we wish for our loved ones at the time of their burial. Light that is life-giving. Light that beatifies. Light that beautifies. Light that is the eternally blissful, infinitely lovely God.

2) And what will the soul see in this light? Before all else it will see itself: it will recognize itself, its faults, its virtues, its merits; it will recognize all this with a clear recognition such as it never attained on earth even by the most careful examination of conscience. What is its permanent value, how far has it succeeded in forming the picture of the eternal God in its soul, for this is the object of earthly life—this it will see at the moment of death with undimmed clearness.

3) And now, dear brethren, do not let us shrink from the task: let us imagine our own souls exposed to this penetrating

light. In it, every past memory, secret longing, hidden wickedness, will be disclosed. What we shall feel is called "the judgment of God."

Everything will come to mind, everything. The dreams of childhood, its desires, virtues, and faults. Words, yearnings, deeds which we thought we had finally forgotten. The years of our youth will come to mind, and the time of betrothal and of young married life.

We shall remember every place we have ever been to: the churches and the places of amusement, the confessionals and the dance-halls, the Eucharistic altar and the saloon bar.

And we shall remember everyone with whom we ever came in contact: our parents, our friends, our children, our husband or wife, our comrades, our accomplices, the fleeting acquaintances of frivolous nights, of sinful friendships kept secret. We will remember those to whom we were a guardian angel, those whom we led into sin. They did not wish to sin, but we persuaded them.

And every word, look, thought; everything we have read, our prayer books, and the indecent magazines, hands clasped in prayer, and thieving hands—everything will be remembered.

The inexorable radiance of perpetual light will be thrown upon our thoughts, words, deeds, glances, and our shortcomings, upon men, places and objects; and this we call "the judgment of God."

C. But what will happen after the judgment?

The judgment was the work of a moment. Of that moment when the ideal picture of what we ought to have become during our earthly life flashed upon us, and next to it appears our marred and disfigured life picture, showing us how in reality we have distorted the divine ideal; this is "the judgment of God."

The judgment upon those who have not realized anything of this ideal, upon whose soul God cannot recognize even the least resemblance to Himself, is final rejection, perdition.

Nevertheless, those upon whose soul glimpses of God's features can be found under all the rubble and dust, are not rejected, but after the improving, restorative work accomplished by purgatorial fire, God receives them into His eternal kingdom.

And if anyone dies who, through grace and his own cooperation, has made reparation here on earth for all his frailty and faults, that is, on his soul shines the resemblance to the divine ideal, in that moment he penetrates the beatifying perpetual light, God's eternal bliss, that we call heaven.

All this happens in a moment; in a shorter time than it takes for a man to lift his hand to throw away a withered flower, or to stretch out his hand to gather a lovely rose, fragrant in the June sunshine.

"It is appointed unto men once to die, and after this the judgment."

My dear brethren. A strange thing happens to the river Rhone in the south of France, on the old boundary line between France and Savoy. Great rocks appear on both sides of the river, coming always nearer and nearer to its banks, until at last they meet above the water so that the river seems to be rushing into a rocky grave where it disappears from sight. The people call the Rhone at this point "the lost river" because it really does disappear from the face of the earth, not even its uproar is audible.

But is this river finally lost? Ah no. On the contrary, under the earth it now accomplishes its most wonderful work. In the bowels of the earth it bores through, and crumbles to dust the granite rocks that bar its way, and when one would think that the earth had finally swallowed it, all at once it bursts forth triumphantly from its rocky grave and its cleansed waters roll on victoriously in the southern sunshine they have once more regained.

At the boundary line of our earthly life we, too, are swallowed up by the grave. The coffin closes down upon us, the river of our lives disappears into the depths of the earth, no sound is heard above the grave. Is our life finally lost? No. Death is only a gate through which we must pass; but beyond the threshold the victorious sunshine of the next world awaits us. Amen.

VII

DEATH VICTORIOUS

In the Berlin National Gallery hangs a startling picture painted by Spangenberg: "The Triumphal Procession of Death."

In the painting, death is seen walking among men, shaking a bell in his bony hand; a vast crowd is following him.

Little children follow him with daisy-chains in their hands, that they had made while playing: but the deathbell interrupted their play and called them away.

A sturdy soldier follows death, the rifle with which he had fought in so many battles still in his hand: but all at once he, too, heard the bell and had to go.

A young girl follows death, her bridal veil falling in soft folds about her face: she heard the bell on her wedding-day and had to go.

Old and young, rich and poor, distinguished and common, are visible in the picture as, accompanied by a flight of crows, they rush unresistingly after death with his bell.

And a helpless old woman, a weary, wrinkled old woman, stretches out her hands longingly toward death, imploring him to take her with him: but he does not want her yet, he leaves her by the wayside.

We read the title under this startling picture: "The Triumphal Procession of Death."

Truly, dear brethren, a picture to make us think. Only from the pulpit can we speak of that painful and affecting reality, of death. Elsewhere people shudder at the thought. Elsewhere they become pale and upset if anyone warns them of the end of earthly life.

But the splendid value of our Christian faith is shown by its not avoiding this most serious question, by its daring to face the serious reality of death, and also by its ability to draw courage and peace even from this depressing fact, from the triumphant procession of death. Christianity clearly points out the startling truth that the fact of death is certain and that the hour of death is uncertain. But it does not make us despair, for at the same time it encourages and consoles us.

Everyone will come to the end of his life, but no one knows when. It is certain that all of us will die, but it is quite uncertain when we shall die. These are two truths that no one can doubt.

I

IT IS CERTAIN THAT ALL OF US WILL DIE

No one can question the fact that all, without exception, are sentenced to death. Holy Writ says clearly: "Remember that death is not slow . . . for the covenant of this world shall surely die" (Ecclus. 14: 12). Whether you are rich or poor, learned or ignorant, healthy or ill, a grayheaded old man or a crying baby in arms, whether you live on land or water, in the temperate or in the torrid zone, working or unemployed: it is all the same. We all shall die. "Remember, man, that thou art dust and into dust thou shalt return," our holy religion says to us on Ash Wednesday.

This is a painful, upsetting truth, but we cannot alter it. Whether we think of it or not, whether we occupy ourselves with it or not, whether we prepare for it or not, some day the Lord will knock at our door. If you have been king, you will die; if you have been pope, you will die; if you have been a poor struggler, you will die. You possess great wealth: do you die too? You do. You are a poor beggar: do you die too? You do.

A. Thousands of years ago in Africa, on the banks of the Nile, mighty pharaohs reigned. Millions bowed abjectly before them. And there beside them were their wives, queens adorned with gold and precious gems, a host of servants waiting to obey their every behest; slave girls combed their long, silky hair. And they also died.

When they died, monuments were erected to them, that were to be worthy of their famous names, where they could sleep their eternal sleep in peace.

This happened four to five thousand years ago. And then? Then archaeologists of the last century discovered these pharaohs' tombs, excavated all their treasures, and the ancient dead are now exhibited in the museums of various cities all over the world.

In any of these museums you may see people standing before a royal mummy in a glass case, looking at it curiously. Are they looking at a king? No. At a handful of dust.

And this ancient corpse looks back at us from its empty eye-sockets that seem as though they were looking from a great distance. And then those compressed lips begin to speak: they tell us a long, ancient story; the beginning chants the hymn of life, speaking to us of pleasures, pomp, and glory. And the end? The end is a softly whispered message: Remember, man, that thou art dust, and into dust thou shalt return.

B. After speaking of the pharaohs, let me speak of other kings. One was Louis XIV, king of France, who is usually called the "sun king" because of his great splendor and magnificence.

He was a favorite of fortune. His armies passed from conquest to conquest. Poets, noblemen, women, one more beautiful than the other, surrounded him with flattery. He built palace after palace. The buildings he erected are counted today among the most beautiful edifices of France. When we see his castle and gardens at Versailles, near Paris, we are speechless in admiration. And he certainly took his share of the good things of life. He did not want to spend a moment without pleasure.

Once, however, someone came. Someone who was mightier and stronger than the "sun king": he struck with the scythe that no one in this world can avoid. And the king was laid to rest in the French royal vaults. Well, gay King Louis, now enjoy yourself. What? You can do so no longer? But you lived for pleasure, King Louis, now amuse yourself. What? You can do so no longer? You cannot even move?

Yet he had one more journey still before him. The French Revolution came and broke open the royal vaults. King Louis' moldering body was also found; on his feet the highheeled shoes that he had worn in life in order to appear taller than he really was. They took his bones, threw them into a great ditch and poured slaked lime upon them, and the bubbling, seething lime seemed to hiss the sad words, "Remember, man, that thou art dust, and into dust thou shalt return."

C. After speaking of pharaohs and kings, shall I also speak of emperors? In the heart of Vienna, the Austrian capital, stands the Capuchin Church. Beneath this building lie the great arched vaults that are the burial-place of the Austrian emperors and Hungarian kings.

Two rows of imposing coffins line the walls: ten, twenty, thirty, who knows their number? There side by side lie emperors, kings, archdukes and archduchesses.

Beneath one great memorial lie Maria Theresa and her husband, Emperor Francis, and their children; after them come the others, right to the latest coffins: to crown-prince Rudolph, Queen Elizabeth I, Francis Joseph. The former possessors of vast temporal power and pomp enclosed in this cold crypt, buried, forgotten, moldering to dust.

When standing there between the coffins of crown-prince Rudolph and Queen Elizabeth, by the statue of the sorrowful Virgin that Hungarian women erected to the memory of Queen Elizabeth, into the deathly silence of the crypt the busy hum of the outer world penetrates, the horns of autos, the clanging of electric street cars, the rumble of carts, the noise of men. Our glance falls on these quiet coffins, and we seem to hear words from their depths, shouted into our ears in that formidable silence: Today you are still king, tomorrow nothing. Remember, man, that thou art dust, and into dust thou shalt return.

D. And shall I speak of the czars? When a Russian czar died, it was the custom to embalm the body, clothe it in a magnificent uniform, lay it in an imposing coffin and place it in the imperial crypt at Petropavlovsk to "eternal rest."

To eternal rest? By no means. The Soviet lords had need of money. They sent a committee down into the realm of deathly silence. One after the other the coffins were broken open.

Alexander III's coffin is broken open. There he lies in his glittering military uniform. From his breast they tear decorations set with diamonds, take from his hand the sword inlaid with brilliants, and hasten to the next coffin. Now it is Alexander II's turn. Now Nicholas I. They come to the coffin of the Czarina Catherine I and tear an immeasurably valuable diamond necklace from the neck of the dead woman. And as the hammerblows of these despoilers of the dead, who are void of all human feeling, ceaselessly resound in the deathly silence, it is again as though we heard the warning cry of transitory life: Remember, man, that thou art dust, and into dust thou shalt return.

E. Shall I give one more example? Yes, but no longer of kings.

Imagine that the world is a hundred years older. It is the middle of the next century. Will this be? Probably. Will there also be frivolous people who live and enjoy themselves and take no thought for their souls? Surely there will be. But who will not be? I shall not be. Nor you. Nor anyone who is here present. We shall then be in our graves, at rest in our graves.

Rest? That is not well said. By that time perhaps our bones will have been exhumed to make place for others. Your house may be still standing, but it will be no longer yours: you will be dust. This church will stand, it will be filled, but you will not be here: you will be dust. Here someone will preach, but it will not be I who do so: I shall be dust. Someone will celebrate mass, but not he who celebrated it today. Young boys will be servers, but not those who served today: those too will already have become dust.

"Oh, death! how bitter is the remembrance of thee" (Ecclus. 41: 1), we could cry in the words of Holy Writ. A dreadful, an appalling thought. One feels uncomfortable, seeks a means of escape, and begins to argue with oneself: "Ah, why are you anxious? True, some day we all have to die. But who knows when that will be?"

II

IT IS UNCERTAIN WHEN WE SHALL DIE

Yet when we try to quiet the unrest of our souls in this way, perhaps we do not even think how very right we are. We are right, but with a difference in emphasis. With a differ-

ence that does not quiet us, but overwhelms us with still
greater despair. "Who knows when death will come?" You
are right: *Who knows when death will come?*

A. One thing is dreadfully certain: that we must die. All
the rest is dreadfully uncertain: when, where, in what manner, in what spiritual state. *Mors certa, hora incerta* says the
inscription on a tower-clock in Leipzig.

1) When shall I die? Perhaps on a sunny day in spring
when the trees are putting forth new leaves and breaking
into blossom. Will they then close my eyes? Shall I fall like
a ripe apple from the tree on a sultry summer day? I do not
know. Will they lower me into the depths of the grave when
the autumn leaves are falling? Or perhaps on a freezing after-
noon in winter when a pall of soft white snow will cover my
grave in a few minutes? I do not know, I do not know.

> "Between the cradle and the grave
> Only one short step is made."

2) And where shall I die?

A shopkeeper once asked a sailor: "Where did your father
die?"

"He was drowned at sea."

"And your grandfather?"

"He was drowned, too."

"And you are not afraid of going to sea?" the shopkeeper
asked in astonishment.

But the sailor replied: "Where did your father die?"

"In bed."

"And your grandfather?"

"He died in bed, too."

"And you are not afraid of going to bed every night?"

Yes, dear brethren: where shall I die? In a quiet room, or

shall I fall dead in the noisy street perhaps? At home or in a hospital? On land or at sea? I do not know.

3) And how shall I die? After long suffering, or suddenly, in a few minutes? In the quiet weakness of old age or in tormenting pain? Surrounded by my relations, or forsaken by everyone? Shall I die a natural death, or in consequence of a railway accident, or perhaps under the wheels of an automobile. I do not know, I do not know.

4) However, after all, dear brethren, this is not important. It is all the same when I shall die and where I shall die and in what manner I shall die, if I can reply to the fourth question: In what spiritual condition will death find me? This is not all the same. Alas, if death should overtake me in sin. This is not all the same.

Yet you will die in the spiritual condition in which you have lived. Death will be only an echo of our lives. We cannot hope that God will perform a miracle for our sakes.

If all our lives we have not received the sacraments, then we cannot hope to receive them at the last moment.

If we have sinned all our lives and have not cared for our souls, if while in health we have not taken time to render a sincere account of our sins in the confessional, then we cannot hope that God will rescue us by a miracle, and that what we neglected to do while in health we can now make amends for while suffering dreadful bodily agony.

No. We cannot hope for this. Our end will be what our lives have been. Alas, if death overtakes us in sin.

B. The postman often brings us mourning-cards that tell us of the death of friends and acquaintances: "It has pleased divine Providence to take our beloved father to his eternal rest after long suffering." Or: "The undersigned announce with sorrowing hearts that . . ." We read these cards with deep emotion, put them aside and—continue our work.

But some day a mourning-card will be printed that you will not be able to read, because your name will stand in thick letters in the center of it. When the postman takes these mourning-cards to their destination, you will be already lying dead in a tiny room. Stiff and cold, and as pale as if you were made of wax. But of all this you will know nothing. Around you relations and friends will be weeping, but you will hear nothing of this.

The priest will come and say to those present: *Oremus pro fidelibus defunctis* ("Let us pray for the faithful departed"). But you will hear nothing of all this: if you lived a good life, well for you; if you died in sin, alas for you.

Slowly the funeral procession will make its way to the cemetery. Once more the sad chant will resound: "Deliver me, O Lord, from everlasting death." But you will not hear this: if you lived a good life, well for you; if you died in sin, alas for you.

The mourners slowly disperse. And you remain there alone in the quiet cemetery. The evening breeze flutters the white veil at the head of your grave. I read the inscription on it: Lived 17 years. So young. Or do I not see well? Lived 71 years? It is all the same. For you it is quite all the same.

Hardly a few years, and you are dust. Time passes over your grave, centuries, millenniums pass. The flowers that bloomed above you have faded long ago. Perhaps a town has been built over the cemetery where you were buried, and in the house erected above your grave people are living; people who laugh as once you did, who are corrupt and wicked, as once you were, who die, as once you did and become dust and ashes: but your soul lives eternally, and as you lived on earth, so your life will be in eternity: if you lived a good life, well for you; if you died in sin, alas for you.

C. We see and feel death's irresistible sway, we see Holy

Writ's words confirmed day by day: "All flesh shall fade as grass and as the leaf that springeth out on a green tree: some grow and some fall off: so is the generation of flesh and blood, one cometh to an end, and another is born" (Ecclus. 14: 18, 19). We experience the truth of this on all sides, yet we see that there are people who still do not believe this. They do not believe that they will also die.

"But that is impossible," you say. "Such a manifestly crazy person does not exist, who would say seriously that he will not die."

Well, that is true, no sane person would say it, but there are many, many millions who live as frivolously, as irresponsibly, as if they believed that they would never die.

Yet I cannot imagine anything more appalling than when someone who does not believe in life everlasting begins to grow old and ill. When such a one has to recognize the fact that the years are passing, that the course of his life is nearly run. And nothing helps, nothing is of any use, rouge is of no use, nor hair-dye, nor the most modern clothes, nor mountain air, nor sea-baths. The end draws ever nearer and nearer, the end of which they never wished to think. And now they see that their hands are empty, alas, dreadfully empty.

D. Now answer one question, dear brethren. If you had to go today? If death should come for you within an hour?

If the Lord should send His angel to you today with the message: "Your stewardship is at an end. Leave everything and come to render your account." What would you do?

Could you reply calmly: "Yes, my Lord, I am ready, everything is in order, I go."

Could you part from everyone with a quiet conscience, and ought you not first to become reconciled to a few with whom you are on bad terms?

Could you part from them forever and ought you not to

restore to them this or that of which you have deprived them?

Could you enter into the Lord's presence with a pure soul and would not your heart be heavy with the memory of many sins committed long ago and still unconfessed?

Could you stand before God: "Father, Thou hast called me, behold Thy faithful child."

Yes? Then all is well. Rejoice and be glad.

But if there is anyone who would be startled by such a message; if there are any to whom it would come unexpectedly and find them unprepared; if there are any with whom not everything is in order, whom this or that neighbor could accuse before God, whose souls are blackened by many sins, unconfessed and unforgiven. I earnestly beg them to put everything in order, to go to confession, to go to confession at once. I beg them not to try God's merciful patience any longer and to think of their unhappy souls.

Let them remember that our earthly lives "are passed away like a shadow . . . and as a ship that passeth through the waves, whereof when it is gone by, the trace cannot be found" (Wis. 5: 9, 10). Let them remember that "life is but wind" (Job 7:7), and "our years shall be considered as a spider" (Ps. 89: 10). Let them remember that "it is not in man's power to stop the spirit, neither hath he power in the day of death" (Eccles 8: 8). Let them remember "if the tree fall to the south or to the north, in what place soever it shall fall there shall it be" (Eccles 11: 3). That is to say, let us remember that it is woe to us if death overtakes us in sin, because as we die so shall we be judged, and as we have lived so we shall die.

My dear brethren. One of the marble memorials in the famous cemetery at Genoa portrays a dead father lying in a coffin. Between the dead father and the weeping girl stands

Christ, His hands raised in benediction above them both, and in the background these three Christian words glitter like a ray of sunshine breaking through from the other world: *Ego sum resurrectio* ("I am the resurrection").

My brethren. We human beings address one another by high-sounding titles, we make becks and bows to one another, we fear one another: yet there are only two truly great powers in the world, two tremendous lords: death and Christ.

Death, who never sleeps, never rests, but mows down his share of human beings day by day: 120,000 persons daily. And wherever these 120,000 funeral processions pass—in villages and towns, on land or at sea—everywhere in the world at sight of them people are deeply affected, they remove their hats, babbling tongues become silent, rosy faces become pale wherever his majesty Death appears.

Death thus reigned supreme for many thousands of years and held his triumphant funeral processions, until 1900 years ago, outside the small town of Naim, one such funeral procession was met by Someone. By Someone who stopped the procession wending its way to the grave, stepped to the young man lying dead on his bier, and said to him: "Young man, I say to thee, arise" (Luke 7: 14). As though some mighty shudder ran through the world, the power of death was broken.

Since then also the years rush by. Since then also funeral bells are tolled on earth. But since then the oppressive knowledge of our brief earthly span of existence no longer weighs so heavily upon us. Since then we know that man's life, however tiny a rivulet of existence it may be, is not swept into the uncertain darkness of oblivion by the rushing years, but the tiny vein of each one's life flows into the limitless ocean of existence that we call God.

Only the rivulet that has accumulated dirt in its passage

through the earth fears the translucent sea. But to those that are able to cast from them the dust and dirt collected on their way and arrive crystal-clear at the crystal ocean, beyond all transiency, beyond every grave, beyond all dissolution, Christ's words will ring out encouragingly, consolingly: "I am the resurrection and the life" (John 11: 25). And Holy Writ's consolation will resound: "Blessed are the dead who die in the Lord" (Apoc. 14: 13); "The souls of the just are in the hand of God" (Wis. 3: 1); "The just shall live for evermore, their reward is with the Lord" (Wis. 5: 16).

My brethren. Let us live as those who know that some day they will die, that we may die as those who know that they will live forever.

Let us live in God's love, that we may die in God's grace. Amen.

VIII

DEATH THE TEACHER

ONE of Christianity's most profound thinkers, most brilliant geniuses, was undoubtedly St. Augustine. His writings contain a large number of original and pithy sayings which crystallize weighty truths. How simple and striking, for instance, are his words, *Sit mors pro doctore* ("Let death be your teacher").

"Doctor Death," "Professor Death"—assuredly a strange idea. Hitherto we have known Professor Jones, Professor Smith, and others, who teach history, political economy, Latin, Greek, chemistry, and so on. But now comes Professor Death. And what subject does he wish to teach? His subject is life; for that is what St. Augustine meant: Let death be your teacher; let death teach you how to live right.

Today, therefore, I take my hearers to this strange professor, to his classroom. Let us listen attentively to what "Professor Death" teaches us. He can speak all languages, and in every land he has a teacher's certificate. Is there an inch of soil in the world where no graves have been dug? Perhaps so. But to find such spots we would have to go to the uninhabited corners of the earth. Wherever there is a grave, there is our professor's rostrum, there sits Death, the great teacher of life. He summarizes his lectures under three headings: Good people, learn of me what a nothingness life is, what a treasure life is, and what a responsibility life is!

84

I

THE NOTHINGNESS OF LIFE

Death's first teaching is this: the nothingness of life.

A. *Sta viator* ("Halt, traveler"), is the warning we read on ancient tombstones. "Pilgrim on earth, halt," is also what death teaches; halt and call to mind how ephemeral everything is, everything. Almighty God alone is eternal.

1) Life flies, quickly it slips from our grasp, however convulsively we would hold it. It is like the flight of an arrow, like a soaring bird. Even if you were to live in a palace and have every luxury that heart can desire, and the best of physicians to treat you with the most expensive remedies, this would all be of no avail.

2) And how uncertain life is! In 1933 an airplane flying from Vienna to Venice crashed. Among its passengers was a young author who suffered serious injuries and died on the evening of the same day. He had flown that day from Berlin to Vienna and after two hours' rest, had continued his flight to Venice. In Vienna he spent the two hours with an acquaintance. They went by automobile to an elegant restaurant. During the meal the young author spoke enthusiastically of the great progress made by technology:

"How powerful the human mind is, after all," he said. "This morning I had breakfast in Berlin; now at noon I lunch in Vienna; this evening I shall dine and listen to the music in one of the restaurants on St. Mark's Square in Venice."

That evening he appeared before the throne of the eternal Judge, and not in a restaurant on St. Mark's Square.

3) "Professor Death" here descends from his professorial chair, goes among the graves, opens them, and makes the dead lying in them to speak.

The young say: "How deceived we were when we counted on a long life and did not believe what we often read inscribed on old clocks: *Jede Stunde bringt die Kunde* ("Every hour something new"). How empty our entire earthly life was! The decades passed like smoke and shadow, and now we see how true the epitaph is that says: *Homo humus, fama fumus, finis cinis,* "man is earth, fame is smoke, the end is dust."

The poor speak and say: "For us death was a release." The rich say: "Not all our wealth was able to save us from this place."

The mighty Macedonian king, Alexander the Great, was right when he commanded that he be placed in his coffin in such a way that his empty hands should hang over the sides of it; let the people see that the mighty king departs with empty hands and can take nothing with him.

Thus the dead speak to us.

"Professor Death," certainly you teach us well.

B. If only your instructive words could be heard by those who live with every fiber of their being for this world only.

1) It is a pity that modern man avoids the thought of death so carefully. He does not like to meet death. The ancient Romans did not fear death. They dug long rows of graves beside the most frequented highways that passersby should see them day by day. Nor did the ancient Christians fear death. Do not think it strange if I say: It would be good for the present-day man to have his attention called to graves sometimes, to visit the sick, the afflicted, and the dead. At every street corner pleasure offers itself: the theater, motion picture theater, dance, bar. In every store, in every fashion display, the world of pleasure offers its wares. Is it any wonder that man forgets there is another world, a world of privation,

suffering, and disease? Is it any wonder that death has to teach those who are unwilling to learn in any other way, that this fleeting life is not true life?

2) And death teaches all this.

It teaches us to be humble, but at the same time confident, too. It teaches us that life is nothing, but at the same time it teaches us what a treasure life is. It teaches us not to become vain, because earthly life is so short; but to be filled with joy because eternal life is so long.

It teaches us that we are citizens of two worlds, but that we cannot find an abiding home in both of them. The visa on our earthly passport authorizes us to "pass through." The permanent domicile to which we are enroute is in the world beyond. Here we are wanderers; in the beyond our permanent home awaits us. Here is the dream, there the reality. Here is the shadow, there the perfection of existence.

3) And then "Professor Death" raises his voice again: Good people; if all this is really so, how can you live as though the contrary were true? How can you live as though your one and only thought were of this world, of daily bread, of business, of pleasure, of the theater, of entertainment? These are your only desires, your only ambitions, your only anxieties. Of what comes after this, of what comes after the sods have fallen with dull thuds upon your coffins, of this truly important, fateful fact you hardly think at all.

A remarkable thing was printed in a certain newspaper published over a hundred years ago. (*Warendorfer Wochenblatt,* July 25, 1835.) It speaks of how a person buried while in a trance could escape if he regained consciousness in the grave. A string must be drawn through a pipe placed in the earth, writes the paper. The string must reach to the dead man's hand, and a bell must be attached to the other end above the earth's surface. If the dead person awakes all he has to do is to pull the string; the consequent signal would at once bring someone to rescue him from the grave.

Are people not strange, dear brethren? It hardly ever happens that anyone is buried in a trance; they want to provide for that remote contingency. It is quite certain, however, that at the moment of death everyone will awake to find himself standing before the judgment seat of God. Yet so many care nothing whatever about this and do not insure themselves for this event.

Let us listen to death's teaching and let us never forget what we are and what we shall become. Our hearts belong to God, not to the world; let us not allow its sins to soil them. Our souls belong to God, not to the world; let us not allow its illusive castles-in-the-air to take us captive. Our gold and our treasures we cannot take into God's presence. Nor our palaces and automobiles. Then what? Only our souls.

The one treasure, the one thing of value that we take with us is our good deeds.

II

THE TREASURE OF LIFE

When "Professor Death" has made us so serious, he produces his second prescription. On the second prescription this is written: Life is short, indeed, but it is also a precious treasure. The past is no longer yours, the future is not yet yours; so use what is yours, use today.

A. The past is no longer yours.

1) Surely no one can see the passing of the years without a bit of sadness on the anniversary of his birthday or on New Year's Eve if he looks back on the years of his life that have flown away so rapidly. How dim every past joy and sorrow,

every task and pleasure, every success and failure, has become. If we look back on our past life, much of it fades into a mist or fog. We still speak of last summer, of a journey we made last spring, perhaps of some greater event. But of what happened several years ago, our memories are, for the most part, vague and dim and uncertain.

2) Time is a mystery. Behind us lies the past; that is no longer ours. Before us lies the future; that is not yet ours. In our grasp we hold the present, a moment of time that slips from our hands even while we grasp it.

Gazing into the darkness ahead, we try, at the beginning of each new year, to see what secrets the future holds. But we can see nothing.

B. We see nothing because the future is not yet ours.

1) How a person encourages and consoles himself: The past year was certainly bitter, but here is the new. In it things must become easier, something unexpected will happen. But time flies past and does not trouble about human beings, neither about those who would like to hasten its flight nor about those who would like to retard it.

The young say impatiently: Oh, if only I could be five years older, if only I had finished my examinations, if only I had my diploma, if only I had a good position. The old say resignedly: If only I were five years younger; then my legs were not so stiff, my breathing was not so difficult, and my hands did not tremble so much. Time does not bother about all that, but rushes on its way.

2) "If only I could know more of the mysterious future. If only I could see what awaits me in life. What danger, what fate, what losses. Why does God not allow us to see into the future?"

So say many people who do not reflect how appalling would be a knowledge of the future. How we might be disheartened, how dreadful it might be to know more of the future than what God has seen fit to impart to us!

The psychological and pedagogical tact shown by Christianity in this question is without its equal. It teaches just so much of our future fate as is necessary to allow us to work with hearts full of hope. Not the merciless blows of an iron-fisted blind fate form our futures, it proclaims, but the fatherly hand of God who provides abundantly for all His children. And His loving heart ordered that we should not know the details of the future awaiting us, that our working strength might not be impaired, that we might not lose courage. We see the final goal where every road ends, but we do not see the road we shall travel. We see only one thing clearly: that at the price of honest endeavor we can gain eternal life.

The past has flown quickly, the future is not yet in my hand; but today is mine. Today I may still love God: I do not know how long I may do so. I may still serve God: but I do not know how long I may do so. Today I may still make reparation for the past: I do not know how long I may do so. Today I may still do penance here for my past sins: but I do not know how long I may do so.

Hence death, at the same time that it shows us the nothingness of life, shows us also what a precious treasure life is. It is a battlefield, an arena, a trial of patience lasting for thirty, fifty, seventy years. On living it rightly depends the whole of life everlasting.

III

THE RESPONSIBILITY OF LIFE

This is death's third teaching: The responsibility of this life.

A. This responsibility makes the hour of death so hard.

1) What hurts us most in death? Is it that we must part from our loved ones, from our sphere of work, from our property? Undoubtedly these things do hurt us. If small children and a widow will be left, the thought of their orphaned state grieves us; if aged parents will be left, their uncertain future causes us grief. If half-finished ambitious plans are left, we are pained to leave the work unaccomplished. If we must leave some laboriously acquired property, the thought of unknown fate pains us. Yet all this is not what hurts us most.

2) Then what is most painful in death? Is it life's final resistance to its passing? Is it the violent disruption of the union of body and soul? This, too, is painful, and for this reason death is bitter. Yet this is not what hurts most in death.

3) Do you know what it is that hurts most? Our life's account that we are now closing, our balance sheet. The hour of reckoning that awaits us. The judgment seat before which we shall presently stand. Our responsibility in God's sight for every word and deed committed during our earthly lives— this is what makes death bitter. The question that stares us in the face: What will happen to us now? Whither shall we go?

What will happen to us? This is what a nervous lady asked when an electric railway car was traveling down a steep mountain side.

"Oh, conductor, what would happen to us if the electric brake should fail to work?"

"Never fear, madam, we still have an automatic emergency brake."

"But what would happen to us if the emergency brake also failed to work?" the passenger nervously asked.

"Well, that would not matter very much either; we would still have the hand-brake."

"But what would happen to us if the hand-brake also failed?"

At that the conductor scratched his head, and answered: "What would happen to us then, madam? Well, some of us would go to heaven and some to hell."

He was right. And in his answer do you not sense the responsibility that rests on each of us? In it we hear our Lord's warning: "Be you then also ready, for at what hour you think not, the Son of man will come" (Luke 12: 40).

B. Now, brethren, reply to my serious question: Are you living in the light of this responsibility? Are your affairs in order? Are you always prepared for death?

For thousands of years people have been dying. Yet death always comes to them unexpectedly. Tell me; if you had to balance your life accounts today, are you prepared to do so? Tell me; are all your affairs in order?

1) Are your money affairs in order? Will there be no contention at your graveside? Have you in your possession nothing that belongs to another? Is no disorder to be found among your obligations? Will not the whole outward appearance of your life collapse at your death, and your relatives have to say at your funeral: "Alas, why did you bring this upon us?"

2) Have you nothing of importance to say to anyone? Tell me; could you really not write that letter today, that letter of explanation, that letter begging forgiveness?

Alas, how much people quarrel with one another! How they embitter one another's lives over trifles! Two bald-headed men are capable of quarreling about a comb. What trifles two brothers can quarrel about! Children and their parents are sometimes estranged for years on account of something utterly insignificant.

All at once death intervenes, and they come to their senses when it is too late.

Recently an old man was buried, and as his relatives made their way home from the funeral they discussed him most touchingly: "What a good man he was, he never harmed anyone." But why did they discover this only after his funeral? Why only after death, when they so often embittered him in his lifetime?

"He was a good man." What a lamentable truth, that many perceive this and say it only when it is too late! How many would be gentler, more forgiving, more forbearing, more loving when it is too late, when it is no longer possible to be so!

3) However, a still more important question arises: Is your soul in order? Do you often think of St. Paul's warning: "Yourselves know perfectly, that the day of the Lord shall so come as a thief in the night. For when they shall say: Peace and security, then shall sudden destruction come upon them" (I Thess. 5: 2, 3).

Mazarin, Louis XIV's great minister, had a stroke of apoplexy while playing cards. "Perhaps it is only a slight indisposition," he thought, and ordered his servant to hold his arm for him that he might continue the game. In vain. The cards fell from his hand and he sank back in his chair. His last words were: "My poor soul, what will become of my poor soul?"

Think of your past life, and you will exclaim: "My poor soul, what will become of my poor soul?"

Into the other mysterious life, into the grave, that long, narrow pit, we can take nothing. Nor can anyone accompany us. Not even our friends, our relatives, our brethren, our parents.

It is dreadful. Then what accompanies us on this uncertain journey? Not our knowledge. Not our good looks, nor our sturdy muscles. Must we stand empty-handed before God?

No, brethren. There is something that accompanies us;

but only one thing. It goes with us to our grave, beyond the grave, right up to the throne of the eternal God, and there it will speak for us.

Who or what is it? Holy Writ, speaking of the dead, says: "Their works follow them" (Apoc. 14:13). Our deeds we take with us.

The glass of water we gave to a thirsty soul, the piece of bread we gave to a beggar, these will go with us and speak for us. Everything we did to help our less fortunate fellow man will accompany us and plead in our behalf. Every kind word and compassionate deed, every comforting glance and loving thought of ours, our struggles to resist temptation, all will accompany us and be our one treasure. "Their works follow them" (Apoc. 14:13).

My dear brethren. If you walk about the streets of Rome, you are made dizzy by the rush of traffic, dazzled by the glittering, splendid life. How many projects, how much endeavor, how much human beauty and brilliance!

When you then ascend one of the seven hills and survey the town from a distance, nothing of this great traffic is seen, no noise is heard, no earthly striving. The houses of this metropolis huddle together like little colored matchboxes. But above them, with reassuring dignity, rises the gigantic cupola of St. Peter's, pointing to the heights.

To such heights today's sermon led: to the heights of "Professor Death's" rostrum, to the heights of the cemetery. If we survey life from these heights, we see how all human striving, planning, and might sink to a little mound of earth on a grave. At such a time it is good to perceive the cupola of our holy faith, rising with comforting calmness above the realm of death.

The thought of death makes everyone shudder. Even be-

lievers? Even those whose sacred hope is that after death life
everlasting awaits them? Is it possible that they, too, fear
death?

Yes, it is possible. The instinct of self-preservation is strong
in every creature, it is life's protecting shield. The body instinctively draws back from disintegration, and however much
anyone thinks of death, however zealous and religious he
may be, he cannot entirely rid himself of this natural dread.
Death was not created by God: sin brought it in its train. Our
human natures fear it and try to escape from it. Hence it is
comprehensible that the life-instinct of even the most devout
believers protests against death and shudders at the thought
of it.

But stronger than the strongest life-instinct is our faith:
death is only a transition from one form of existence to another, when we cast off one worn garment and put on a new
one in its stead, "that that which is mortal may be swallowed
up by life" (II Cor. 5: 4). Death is not a sinking into nothingness, into Nirvana, but the beginning of real life. Here we
walk in shadow, there in sunshine; here in strife, there in
God's peace; here in a foreign land, there in the Father's
house; here we believe, there we know.

This belief does not allow us to despair, but teaches us to
pray:

Dear Lord, I beg, if it is good in Thy sight, let not my death-
struggle be torturing. If it is good in Thy sight, let not my
fear of death be tormenting. If it is good in Thy sight, let
not death overtake me in a strange country, where I am alone.
All this I beg, my Lord.

But more than all else, one thing I beg. Do not allow death
to overtake me without my having made my confession,
without my having received the sacraments, without my having gained Thy pardon. Allow me after my last communion

to repeat with a tranquil soul the aged Simeon's words: "Now Thou dost dismiss Thy servant, O Lord, according to Thy word in peace" (Luke 2: 29). And that I may then add: "Father, into Thy hands I commend my spirit" (Luke 23: 43); and as an echo hear Thy words: "Well done, good and faithful servant, because thou hast been faithful over a few things, I will place thee over many things; enter thou into the joy of thy Lord" (Matt. 25: 21). Amen.

IX

THE WARNING OF DEATH

HAVE you ever stood at the middle of a bridge when great blocks of ice were being swept under it by the water? If you have not, sometime stand on a bridge when the river is covered with masses of floating ice and look fixedly at the drifting ice. You need not look long; at once you will feel that the bridge is moving under you and that you are being swept away by the current, and you will almost clutch the railing of the bridge to prevent yourself from being drawn away.

This feeling of uncertainty takes possession of our souls as often as we think of the transient character of all things human, of life's hurrying river, as often as we think of death; as often as we feel how the boundless ocean of time sweeps the swiftly rolling waves of life under us. At such times we feel as though we, too, were being swept along helplessly by the current, and instinctively we take refuge in the belief in eternal life, the only sure support to which mortal man can cling.

However earnest and honest our lives may be, we cannot deny that we Christians are deeply touched by the passing of time. We, too, are shaken by the knowledge that death is inevitable. We do not, however, let this mood become foolishly sentimental, but strive to understand the admonition it contains. Death admonishes us of our responsibility and of our duty.

97

I

THE PASSING OF TIME

As often as we see death's harvest around us we, too, feel
the icy breath of things transient. At such times we see the
truth of psalm 101: "In the beginning, O Lord, Thou foundest the earth, and the heavens are the works of Thy hands.
They shall perish but Thou remainest; and all of them shall
grow old like a garment, and as a vesture Thou shalt change
them, and they shall be changed. But Thou art always the
selfsame and Thy years shall not fail" (Ps. 101: 26–28). How
true this psalm is!

A. Everything becomes old and changes.

1) The whole universe in which we live becomes old. The
earth grows old and changes, the heavenly bodies grow cool,
the warmth of the sun decreases. A decade or a century does
not count much in the life of the universe, but the unceasing
passage of centuries and millenniums counts. The earth and
all the created world gradually grows old.

2) Of course many people do not take this very tragically.
The sun is growing old and will sometime become cold. Well,
let it. The earth is growing old and sometime the fuel supply
will be exhausted. Well, it will be exhausted. All this would
not cause us anxiety, if we did not perceive something else
as well. We cannot perceive that the earth and the sun are
growing older, but we see something else most plainly; we
see that people grow old: our friends and relations; and we
see that we, too, are growing old.

"Oh, how many gray hairs you have!" we exclaim when
we meet some friend whom we have not seen for six months
or so.

"Where have you been that you are all dressed up?" we ask.

"I have been to Charlie's wedding."

"Is he already a married man? I used to play with him when he was a little fellow in short pants. How old we are getting!"

Yes, we are growing old. Everything changes and grows old like a garment.

B. But Thou, O Lord, art always the selfsame, and Thy years shall not fail. Only God does not grow old. With God "there is no change nor shadow of alteration" (James 1: 17). "Before the mountains were made, or the earth and the world was formed, from eternity and to eternity Thou art God" (Ps. 89: 2). "For a thousand years in Thy sight are as yesterday which is past" (Ps. 89: 4).

Hence it is a beautiful custom that, when hurrying autos and crowded streetcars pass a church, men who are jostling one another in the struggle to make a livelihood, become silent for a moment and raise their hats or make the sign of the cross. At such times ephemeral man pays respect to the only eternal God.

When everything around us decays and the screech-owl voice of destruction screams at us on all sides, then we turn to this eternal God and grasp His hand more firmly. We, who are but short-lived, weak creatures, we trust in the God who is always the selfsame and whose years shall not fail. We trust in the God who was mighty enough to call this stupendously vast world into existence from the void. We trust in the God who was mighty enough to keep it in existence for thousands and thousands of years. We trust in the God without whose knowledge not a hair of our heads is harmed and not a sparrow falls.

Therefore we must not be weakly sentimental at the sight of death's dominion. It should bring two things to our minds: our responsibility and our duty; our responsibility with regard to earthly life, and our duty with regard to God.

II

DEATH WARNS US OF OUR RESPONSIBILITY

The first thought that takes possession of us at the sight of death is one of responsibility for the account we must some day render.

A. My life is a book, every page is a year. And after I have completed my life on earth, this book will be opened in heaven. The book is "the book of life" (Apoc. 20: 12), in which everything is written.

1) Everything. How appalling only to think of it! Every word, act, and thought of mine, that perhaps I have forgotten long ago, is written down. Yet it will be so. Our blessed Lord repeatedly warns us that He will demand a reckoning from us.

A wealthy man makes big plans for the future: he will eat, drink, and be merry. But God says to him: "Thou fool, this night do they require thy soul of thee." "Give an account of thy stewardship" the Lord says to His steward in one of His parables. On another occasion He speaks of the talents that He will demand back with interest (Matt. 24: 14 ff.). Again at another time, of the barren fig tree: He will wait one year longer for it to bear fruit; but if it does not do so then, He will cut it down and cast it into the fire (Luke 13: 6 ff.).

2) Aware of this responsibility, how differently I will direct my whole earthly life! I will certainly bear in mind the answer given by an English missioner to an opulent business man. The priest was invited to dine with a certain rich man.

But even during dinner the telephone bell rang repeatedly, and the host arranged several transactions.

"You see, father," he said, "here in this house, no time at all is lost."

"Time, indeed not," replied the missioner, "but Eternity, I fear."

B. If, aware of this, I want to survey the results of my stewardship, if I look to see whether the talent God entrusted to me has brought interest; if I seek the fruit on my tree of life, I wonder what the result of the accounting will be at the end of my life.

1) We are acquainted with the modern cash registers with which large stores are equipped. Each smallest payment is typed on a tape of paper. In the evening, at the pressure of a button, the total of the whole day's receipts lies before us most precisely added together.

But what is this accurate cash register compared to God's "bookkeeping," compared to the book which Holy Writ mentions when it says: "And I saw the dead, great and small, standing in the presence of the throne, and the books were opened . . . and the dead were judged by those things which were written in the books according to their works" (Apoc. 20: 12). I look back upon my past life: must I not be startled when I think of the precise bookkeeping in the next world?

2) An exhibition of pictures was visited by someone who stood about in the galleries, bored and uninterested, because even the most beautiful pictures made no impression on him. When he began to complain to one of the artists how tiresome the exhibition was, the artist replied: "If only I could lend you my eyes, dear friend."

How differently we should look at an exhibition of pictures, if we could borrow an artist's eyes! And how differently we should look at this world too, at life, at all our earthly struggles and plans, if we could borrow the eyes of a saint! Let us say the eyes of St. Aloysius; the eyes of the St. Aloysius who put this question to himself before every undertaking: "Of what use will this be to me in gaining eternity?" Or if we could borrow St. Paul's eyes, the eyes of the St. Paul who wrote: "I reckon that the sufferings of this time are not worthy to be compared with the glory to come, that shall be revealed in us" (Rom. 8: 19). Or if we could borrow the eyes of the Lord Jesus Himself, the eyes of our Lord who said: "For what doth it profit a man if he gain the whole world and suffer the loss of his own soul?" (Matt. 16: 26.) This is the feeling of responsibility that comes from the thought of death.

Can we, with the valuable material placed in our hands, form such an image of our soul that God's eyes will rest with delight on its beauty? It does not depend on us whether this image shows an old man or a young boy, an aged woman or a young girl. How much time on earth God intends to give to each one, is His secret. But it depends on us and we are responsible whether the soul of the old man or young boy, the old woman or the young girl, is beautiful or not.

III

DEATH WARNS US OF OUR DUTY

The knowledge of this responsibility arouses in us a sense of duty. A double duty: to show a filial gratitude to God for the love He has bestowed on us, and to make a manly decision about the future.

A. The moments in which our thoughts are occupied with death are also the moments in which to give thanks to God. Perhaps never can we say the first words of the preface at mass with so much feeling as in these moments: *Vere dignum et justum est,* "It is truly meet and just, right and available to salvation, that we should always and in all places, give thanks to Thee, O holy Lord, Father almighty, eternal God." We give thanks for all the good that Thou hast bestowed on us in life till now, but we give thanks also for every affliction with which Thou hast visited us.

1) To give thanks for all good bestowed on us. Before all else I give thanks to God for the spiritual favors I have received during my prayers, especially during mass and through the reception of the sacraments. I give thanks for all the loving pardon granted to me after my many backslidings. For the immeasurable love that entered into my heart with the Holy Eucharist. For all the grace that aided and guided me even though I was unaware; that saved me from so many falls which I shall know about only in the next world. For all this I give humble thanks.

But then I also wish to give thanks for all material blessings bestowed on me: for health and a livelihood, for my family and my friends, for my successes, for my recovery from illness. Gratitude for favors received is dictated by our instinctive human feeling.

2) Nevertheless we must be grateful also for the suffering and trials that God has visited upon us in the course of our lives. Many people find this hard to understand.

A few years ago everybody was infected by the crossword-puzzle fever. It was a sort of intellectual epidemic. Husband and wife at the dinner table, clerks and storekeepers at their desks and behind the counter, schoolchildren of all ages—all were solving crossword puzzles. Yet for those who did not understand them, these puzzles were nothing but horizontal and vertical rows of letters and a confusion of black squares lying mixed pell-mell. For those who did not understand them. But for the initiated, behind the black lines, seeming to run aimlessly hither and thither, an interesting and intelligible solution lay hidden.

Earthly life puts everyone face to face with difficult and often bitter crossword puzzles. If only more people understood the solution of their crossword puzzle. If only everyone possessed the necessary skill and patience. In the lives of those who do not understand it, the black lines of disaster and trial run in aimless confusion; whereas those who understand it, know that in the eyes of God every black line has its meaning and purpose.

What a pity that many do not even wish to understand this! Yet this is the truly Christian concept: to say *Te Deum* also in failure. To say *Te Deum* also in sickness. To say *Te Deum* also in poverty. It is chiefly of this that St. Paul admonishes us: "Giving thanks always for all things, in the name of our Lord Jesus Christ, to God and the Father" (Eph. 5: 20).

B. Besides gratitude, the thought of life's brief span makes me aware of another obligation: the duty of manly decision. If everything rushes toward death, if everything sooner or later slips from our grasp—health, good looks, money, pleasure, fortune, rank, fame, everything—then henceforth our all will be, not this world, but life everlasting; the world and worldly possessions will be only means toward life eternal.

1) During his imaginary journey, when Dante arrived at the gate of Paradise, before entering he glanced back once more at the earth. "I looked back across the seven spheres," he writes. "I saw the earth: it was so small that I had to smile at sight of it. So that is the little place that often makes us so proud."

Does not the same feeling possess us when, in the last moments of a passing year, we look back at it as it prepares to sink into its grave? How the past twelve months, fifty-two weeks, three hundred and sixty-five days shrink! Was that the year that so often made us proud, foolhardy, sinful?

For many people this earth is everything. This earth and its pleasures, its wealth, its treasures. "He who has money, has everything," they say.

Yet indeed it is not so. With money you purchase things to eat, but not an appetite. With money you can purchase medicine, but not health. You can buy soft pillows, but not quiet sleep. You can buy a beautiful house, but not a good conscience. You can buy acquaintances, but not friends. You can buy servants, but not their loyalty. And principally, with money you can buy a beautiful crypt in the cemetery for your body; but a place for your soul in life everlasting? No. A thousand times no.

Then let us be wise, dear brethren. You know the reproach that was once made to the great astronomer, Tycho Brahe, by his coachman: "Good master, you know your way about the heavens, but here on earth you are very stupid."

How many modern people would deserve this reproach, but reversed: "You know your way about the earth very well, you are quite at home here, but you are stupid with regard to heaven, you do not trouble about your eternal home and your destiny."

2) We still have time, God has left us the continuation of our lives. Do not let us waste that too. You know what St. Augustine wrote of the value of time: Moments are the seeds of eternity, he said (*semina aeternitatis*). Time is precious, for with time well used we can purchase eternity.

The years pass, flying by one after the other in rapid succession. Sad it would be if, at the end of a life that has sped by all too quickly, we should have to exclaim with Hebbel: "The man I am, sorrowfully greets the man I might have been."

In describing some ancient churches, Baedecker's guide books often remark: "It is regrettable that the frescoes were later retouched." A regrettable barbarism: to ruin a masterpiece with bungling strokes of the brush. But Christianity has imprinted such a masterpiece upon our souls: Christ's divine features. Let us be watchful that sin does not daub its vileness upon this masterpiece. If this misfortune has happened in the past, let us be the more watchful henceforth. Time is passing. We must not postpone the work of repair and restoration.

If even after our best intentioned resolves we become aware that we waver again and again, and if after another fall we again have to lift our hands in supplication for pardon, even then we must make a fresh start, a thousand times if need be. Let our consolation be the knowledge that when we appear before the omniscient God, He not only knows our faults and failings but also our many brave exertions and struggles in trying to overcome them. True, He sees our falls, but He sees also our repentance.

This earth is a vale of tears for all of us. Like an endless line of pilgrims, humanity winds its way through it, and every pilgrim—great or small, rich or poor, young or old, man or woman—every pilgrim carries his own cross upon his shoulder. Right through all the stations of life until we arrive. For the pilgrimage has an end. We shall arrive.

Now if everything in this world passes away, are we not foolish to build our lives on something so transient? In your room do you not hear time steadily sawing at your tree of life? Each tick of the clock is a movement of the saw under your feet.

Is any man so foolish as to build himself a beautiful house on quicksand, on a boggy swamp? We build with concrete, and reinforced concrete at that. Eternity, that is reinforced concrete. Eternity, that is a foundation on which we can build confidently.

Brethren. The stream of time sweeps the ice-blocks of the years beneath us; but we have a strong support to which we can cling: our belief in eternity.

And if in the midst of such thoughts we can listen to death's warning, then at the hour of our departure the promise of the psalm will be fulfilled in us: "He that dwelleth in the aid of the most High, shall abide under the protection of the God of Jacob. He shall say to the Lord: Thou art my protector, and my refuge; my God, in Him will I trust (Ps. 90: 1, 2). Amen.

X

THE SOBERING FACT OF DEATH

On the last day of the year usually a great deal of business is done at the post office. The postmen can hardly cope with the work. Small envelopes, big envelopes, picture postcards, and greetings. Almost all of them have the same contents: "Wishing you a happy New Year." A happy year. Happier than last year. This is an agreeable custom. It may well be, of course, that the good wishes will not make the new year a happy one.

Some try to insure a happy new year by other means. They start the new year by not going to bed that night. Friends and relatives gather and wait for midnight. When the clock strikes twelve they clink glasses and greet one another with, "A happy New Year." Of course the new year will not be happier because of this.

Others do something else. Restaurants and cafes are filled to overflowing by those who have not learned to enjoy themselves at home. When midnight comes they raise a din with shouting, singing, blowing horns, and the like, and cry out almost hysterically: "Happy New Year." Of course the new year will not be any happier because of all this.

But, dear brethren, when our holy religion repeatedly and emphatically admonishes us of the importance of this brief earthly life, she does so to insure us a genuinely happy life. Not only does she wish it for us, she also tells us how to obtain it. Courageously facing us—men who are to forget all

else in the preoccupations of everyday life—she cries into our
ears unpopular and sobering truths: "Good people, call to
mind how brief earthly life is, and how important earthly life
is. If you use life properly, then indeed it will be happy and
blessed for you.

I

THE BREVITY OF EARTHLY LIFE

A. How short life is! When a man is born, a lighted candle
is, as it were, placed in his hand. He knows that the candle
is burning, that its length is steadily decreasing, and that
some day it will flare up for the last time. But no one knows
how long his candle will last.

When a man is born, he starts out on a journey, but he does
not know how long this journey will be. He knows that it
will lead up and down hill, sometimes in sunshine, sometimes
in storm; and some day he will reach the end of the road. But
no one knows at what moment he will reach there.

How short life is! Like the skilful extraction of a tooth: the
patient is in tense expectation; now, now is the moment, but
by that time the tooth is out. By the time we notice it, the
greater part of life is past, it is no longer in our hands. "Have
I really lived so long?" we sometimes ask wonderingly. Little
children often say: "When I am grown up." The young still
see visions and build magnificent castles-in-the-air. Adults,
however, become more modest, year by year their aircastles
are less sumptuous. Some fine day we notice that we are saying: "When I was young."

How short life is! The Bible reiterates again and again:
"The days of man are short, and the number of his months is
with Thee: Thou hast appointed his bounds which cannot
be passed" (Job. 14: 5). "Behold Thou hast made my days

measurable, and my substance is as nothing before Thee. And indeed all things are vanity, every man living. Surely man passeth as an image" (Ps. 38: 6, 7). "Man's days are as grass, as the flower of the field so shall he flourish; for the spirit shall pass in him and he shall not be, and he shall know his place no more" (Ps. 102: 15, 16).

B. Although life is so short, we do not relish facing the fact. On the contrary, a strange, disillusioning, unpleasant feeling comes over the man deeply immersed in daily cares, when he finds himself face to face with the brevity of life.

1) Yet often we meet with death. Burdened with care, weaving plans for the future, we hasten along the busy streets of the city, and all at once we meet a funeral procession. Someone has died. Someone who hurried along these streets a few days ago with just as many cares, with just as many plans as we do now. What a disturbing encounter!

We walk in flowery meadows in the warm sunshine of a May day. A sweet fragrance fills the air, everything is sheer beauty, sheer joy. Suddenly we start back: the lifeless body of a little bird lies before us on the ground. Even here death and corruption have accompanied us.

A beautiful red apple is set before you at the end of dinner. We cut it in half: it is full of worms. Even here we find death and corruption.

2) We meet death on all sides, but never does it seem so dreadful, so tangible, so audible as on the last day of the year, on New Year's Eve. Then we can almost see how the present becomes the past; we can almost hear how the current of the year flows into the shoreless ocean of time.

During the year a man is as immersed in his work as a schoolboy in some interesting book that falls into his hands: he sees nothing except the book.

We adults, too, are wholly preoccupied during the year

with the struggle for life, with duty and work. We toil and strive in the race for success. But on that evening when, as it were, we hear the creaking of the wheels of passing time, when we almost feel its transitory character, on that evening the question arises: Why, why? Every flower at last fades. Every child grows old. Morning is followed by night. Every summer passes into winter.

At such times we ask ourselves a painful question. A question which always abides in the depths of our souls, but which in that hour burns with tormenting pain: Is it true that we also must some day die? Is man like the year now hastening toward its grave: a little surging of the waves, a ruffling of the water; and then silence, a final passing on?

3) When we have experienced all this, when this thought has made us humble, when the dreadful burden of it has almost overwhelmed us, then we take the first step toward true greatness, toward real life, toward genuine values— toward a really happy new year. Whoever has once looked with seeing eyes upon the brevity of earthly life and into the infinity of eternity, becomes serenely tranquil, and his peace cannot be taken from him.

This happened to St. Francis of Assisi when he fell seriously ill at twenty-three years of age, and looked death in the face. He did, in fact, recover, but the whole world became dim and shadowy in his eyes; he heard the voices of his old friends, but with only half an ear; he saw the world he had been used to, but he now saw with penetrating eyes: his eyes, bathed in the light of eternity, saw behind all earthly vanity the skeleton of its ephemeral character. This trail St. Paul mentions when he says: "We have not here a lasting city, but we seek one that is to come" (Heb. 13: 14).

"But if we think like that, earthly life will lose its purpose and meaning." No, indeed.

On the contrary: after we think like that, earthly life gains a new purpose and a higher meaning. True, everything passes, but everything returns to the hand of its maker, God. In this sense life is truly eternal circulation: it starts from God's hand and returns to God's hand.

Thus we arrive at the second sobering lesson: earthly life is short; but it is not only short, it is also important.

II

THE IMPORTANCE OF LIFE

Happy the man who takes to heart the admonition that life is not mere pleasure, not mere work. It is something besides this, it is also the service of God.

A. Life is mere pleasure. Anybody's heart is grieved when he reads in the newspapers about almost incredible instances of a frivolous squandering of life; when he notes how irresponsibly some persons waste their whole earthly life. If anyone mentions the matter to them directly, they are offended. "Oh, leave me in peace. A man lives only once," they say in a tone of rebuke.

If they would but consider what they are saying: A man lives only once. Since you live only once, it is more important than anything else that you live this one life well. If you had two lives, you might perhaps risk one of them. But you have not two lives, you have only one life. This you must live well. Life is something more than pleasure seeking. And it is not the sort of "happy new year" that our holy religion wishes us.

B. Life is not merely work. It is indeed toil; but not only that. It is a struggle for bread; but not only that. It is a hard struggle with the cares of earning a livelihood; but not only that.

How hard the present-day man works. If we consider the

daily labor of a man engaged in a trade, of a physician, a lawyer, a professor, a business man, a laborer, we see what a rush their life is. A mother, a typist, a woman at any kind of work, a teacher; they have to perform racking work. But this in itself is still not the ideal of Christian life. It is still not the "happy new year" that our holy religion wishes us.

C. If life is not merely pleasure and not merely work, what else is it? What is this happy and harmonious life? Most people would certainly be confused if on New Year's Day we were to say to them: "A few moments ago you wished me a happy new year. Now what precisely do you mean by a happy new year?"

"What do I mean? That you may enjoy good health."

O yes: good health is a treasure. But it is only a part of happiness. For if it were happiness itself, then people who are in splendid health would not complain of unhappiness.

"A happy new year? Why, I wish you financial success and prosperity; that will make the new year a happy one."

But this will not make it a happy year. True, without money we cannot live. But to live happily with nothing but abundance of money is equally impossible. We see that often those who have great wealth sink into the most appalling morass of immorality. And we see that those who in despair take their lives are not always people who live in poverty. Money leads to dissension among relatives, money arouses sinful passions. No, money does not insure happiness.

"Well then, I wish you abundance of pleasures in the new year: visits to the theater, dances, an automobile, fur coat. Surely that is enough."

Enough? It is by no means enough! Something within us begins to speak after the emptiness of nights spent in pleasure. Within us is a voice that can be silenced for a time, but that at length cries out in protest. You return home from attending a funeral, or you are crushed by some calamity, or you are sitting alone at home, with nothing to break the silence but the ticking of the clock. Then this voice begins to speak. We are possessed by a great longing that not all the pleasure in the world can satisfy. We are possessed by a homesickness that all the treasures of this world cannot satisfy.

We shall insure ourselves a happy new year, a happy life, if we hear this voice and heed it. Our life will be a happy life if we satisfy this longing. Our life will be a happy one if we appease this yearning. As the years pass, every other voice within us becomes quieter, every longing of ours becomes weaker, every other road leads us rather into the mists, but the voice of eternal life rings out, the longing for life everlasting flares up.

D. Now I understand what a happy life is. It is something more than pleasures, something more than work; a happy life is the service of God. Whoever you are, wherever you are, of whatever age you are, whatever position you are in: your life must be in the service of God.

How will it become a service of God, you ask. By praying morning and night? By going to mass on Sunday and keeping the fast days? By frequently going to confession and communion? By doing all these things.

Is something further necessary? Yes indeed. We must fulfil our duty wherever Providence has placed us. We must be strict with ourselves and forbearing with others. We must firmly control the corrupt instincts latent within us and must be willing to journey by the hard and rugged road that leads to God. We must consider this life only as a temporary sojourn, and seek the answer to its every question by the light of eternity.

Brethren. This is the secret of a happy life. Whether you are a child or an adult, a father or a mother, a young man or a young woman, let your life be a service of God. You may also enjoy earthly life, in the right way. You must also work during your earthly life, perhaps a great deal. But besides all this, besides enjoyment and work, do not forget that the candle in your hand is always burning down, the path ahead of you is always growing shorter, life is slipping from your grasp. Take care, then, that you do not have to appear before God's judgment seat with empty hands.

Your life will be happy if, besides the many, many transient earthly tasks, you also accomplish a work that reaches over into eternity. Your life will be happy if day by day you make your memorial more beautiful. For that is everyone's task: to work out a memorial for himself. It is not important whether this memorial is the statue of a child or a youth, a young man or an old man, but that it should please the eternal God. This is important, that in it the eternal God may recognize His own image.

III

THE VALUE OF LIFE

Here the third great admonition falls on our ears: This life is short, this life is important, then use this life to the best of your ability, turn the coming years to the best account. Our ancestors had a fondness for putting abstract religious truths into graphic narrative form. Thus originated the ancient story of a poor simple man who is sitting alone in his hut on New Year's Eve when, precisely as the clock strikes twelve, an angel appears and places a sack of gold in front of him, saying: "This is yours. Use it well. Be happy with it." The angel disappears. At first the poor man is speechless with astonishment, wondering whether he is awake or dreaming. Finally seeing that the affair is no jest, he says: "With this money I will first of all pay my debts, then I will be very careful how I use the remainder."

The poor man who receives a sack of gold on New Year's Eve is, properly speaking, ourselves. The remainder of life that we receive from divine Providence is a great asset, an immense treasure. What shall we do with it? Pay our debts and take care how we use the remainder.

A. Before all else I will use the remainder of my life to pay my debts: the many debts to God I made in my past life. "Many pay with a chronic illness in the second half of their lives for the sins they committed in the first half," said an experienced physician. This thought is continued by Christianity. In their life after death men pay for all the sins they committed in their life before death.

I must be grateful to God that He has given me the opportunity to pay my debts, the opportunity to repent, to confess, to atone here in my earthly life. I may not say: I still have plenty of time.

You have time? Brethren, time deceives us. Every day time shows us a new dawn, but moments that have passed never return. Time never stands still. "The number of days that we have lived are so many steps nearer to our goal. The older we are, so much shorter is the remainder of our lives" (St. Gregory). "See therefore, brethren, how you walk circumspectly not as unwise but as wise, redeeming the time" (Eph. 5: 15).

You have time? On December 24, 1933 an awful railway accident occurred near Paris. In a moment of time this accident took more than two hundred people—many of them children traveling home for the holidays—before the judgment seat of God. At the scene of the collision, the railroad line was strewn with broken toys. But perhaps the most dreadful relic was a bloodstained school-report containing the following: "He is very quick-witted, intelligent, diligent; a great future awaits him." The boy was lying among the dead. "A great future awaits him." Do not say, my brethren, that you still have plenty of time.

You have time? If the dead were to return, what would they wish for? Gold? Automobiles? Theaters? Champagne? Only a little time. Not even a year, a month. "If only we had a week in which to pay our debts to God." Brethren, pay your debts as soon as possible in a sincere holy confession.

B. What shall I do with my life henceforth, with the treasure that God has given into my hands? Besides paying my past debts, I will make a wise use of it.

Look back upon your past life, simply upon the last year, and ask yourself this question: "Can I be satisfied?" But take care what you reply. There are some who will hasten to reply: I am satisfied. This year I passed my examinations; I married; I found a position. I bought a little house. My savings have increased.

Take care. These things you do not take with you. And if you stand before your Judge, and He asks: "Is that all you have brought with you?" You will have to answer: "That is all." You open your hands: they are empty, quite empty.

I do not want to make such use of the time that is still mine. I wish to make good use of it, that at the end of each day I may be able to say at my night prayer: My Lord, today I not only became older, I not only came nearer death, but I also came a step nearer to Thee. I became one degree better. One fault of mine I have vanquished. I have added another stroke to the picture of our Lord in my soul and made it a trifle more beautiful.

My brethren. With such elevating and reassuring thoughts the Christian confronts the inexorable power of death. Our life's candle is burning down. Earthly paths become shorter in front of us. Life slips more and more from our grasp. It is man's fate that he must go. Not out into the dark and gloomy night, but into the waiting arms of God. It is man's fate that the river of his life flows on and passes. Not into a parched lake, but into the infinite ocean of eternal life.

Today the praise given to God by the psalmist is still valid: "In the beginning, O Lord, Thou foundest the earth, and the heavens are the works of Thy hands. They shall perish, but Thou remainest; and all of them shall grow old like a garment and as a vesture Thou shalt change them and they shall be changed. But Thou art always the selfsame, and Thy years shall not fail" (Ps. 101: 26–28).

And St. Paul's words to the Thessalonians also remain valid: "To you who are troubled, rest with us when the Lord Jesus shall be revealed from heaven with the angels of His power in a flame of fire, giving vengeance to them who know not God and who obey not the gospel of our Lord Jesus Christ. Who shall suffer eternal punishment in destruction from the face of the Lord and from the glory of His power, when He shall come to be glorified in His saints and to be made wonderful in all them who have believed" (II Thess. 1: 7–10).

Brethren, life is like a banknote: it is not valuable in itself but for what can be purchased with it. We are still in a position to purchase eternal bliss with our use of life. We are still in a position to avoid coming among those whom God will condemn to eternal punishment in hell; we can still come among those whom He will praise and receive into His eternal realm. Amen.

XI

DEATH THE GUIDE

CHRISTIANITY shows courage in keeping one day of the year as "All Souls Day" and taking the living among the dead on that day. General opinion and practice regard all mention of death as something tactless, unseemly, indelicate.

How peculiar are human ways of thought! Life's greatest admonition, most moving truth, and most inevitable reality is death. Yet it is seldom mentioned except by euphemism.

Day after day the postman delivers black-bordered mourning-cards, the newspapers contain several accounts of sudden death; in every large city cemetery many burials take place every day: yet we bury our heads in the sand because we dread to face the reality.

But not all of us. On some tombs you may see carved a broken pillar or an inverted and extinguished torch. But we Christians, who place the cross of hope on the graves of our loved ones, have no reason to avoid reflection on this earnest and moving truth. The thought of the other world is indeed serious and solemn, but it is not without hope and comfort.

Is death's realm shrouded in gloom? Do mournful sorrow and fear wander among the graves in the cemetery? Or do warm sunbeams of consolation and encouragement shine forth from this other world? The sunlight contains ultraviolet rays which are more invigorating than the others. Invisible to the human eye, they can be detected by especially sensitive mechanisms. Likewise to the materially-minded the sadness of the cemetery is dark and forbidding; but to the sensitive eyes of faith that saddenness is lighted with the radiance of belief in life everlasting.

In the tombs of the ancient Egyptian pharaohs grains of wheat were placed. Recently these grains, discovered when the tombs were opened, were planted in the soil and, after these thousands of years, they sprang into verdant life. Like this seed, is belief in life beyond the grave, seed that is sown by religion in the graves and springing into blades of blessed consolation.

This light from the other world gives us a different view of earthly life and helps us to bear life's hardships.

I

A DIFFERENT VIEW OF EARTHLY LIFE

A. We are oppressed at the thought of a grave without a cross above it.

1) We struggle all our life, and at the end what remains? The certainty that we must go! Were I an animal, this thought would not disturb me. Horse and rider go together into battle, to suffering and death. But the horse never asks, Why? Why all this? Only the rider does that.

A child stands on the curbstone. He has a cake in his hand from which he takes huge bites, at the same time crying bitterly. "Why are you crying, little boy?" a passerby asks. "I am crying," answers the boy, "because every time I take a bite, my cake gets smaller." Certainly there is something to cry for in that. Thus life, too, decreases in our hands as each passing hour takes a bite out of it.

2) But this thought saddens only those who have no ray of sunshine from the other world. For it is our sacred conviction that the grave is merely the final station of a state of

earthly existence, but not the annihilation of life itself. Thus with eyes of faith I see this earthly life and its tasks in another light. I set myself other goals, I make other plans, have other desires, other tasks. I do not value life too highly, but neither do I undervalue it. I do not want to obtain its pleasures and comforts at any cost, even at the cost of sacrificing my moral principles. Strictly speaking, this alone is real death: the destruction of spiritual values, the extinguishing of the fire of the Holy Ghost in our souls.

B. But does the thought of the rapid passing of life diminsh our love of work? On the contrary, it stimulates it. You need only look at the haymakers when a summer thunderstorm threatens to break above their heads. With industrious haste they redouble their efforts that they may gather in the hay before the rainfall. Our earthly life is such a haymaking and harvesting.

A certain author writes: "If on January first we could be certain that we would die on the next December thirty-first, how different our way of thought, our work, our behavior would be! How much excitement we would consider useless; how much more kindly we would regard others; how grateful we would be for a short spell of lovely weather, for a good suit, for a plate of food! How little we would be concerned about the political situation or the Stock Exchange!

C. Belief in life hereafter is also a connecting link between the living and the deceased members of a family. Thus says St. Paul: "Be not sorrowful, even as others who have no hope" (I Thess. 4: 12).

This belief rings forth from Christ's words of comfort inscribed over the graves of our dear ones: "He that believeth in Me, although he be dead, shall live" (John 11: 25).

This belief carries our love beyond the grave, finding expression not only in the placing of wreathes on the graves of our dear ones, but rather in prayers said for them, in masses offered for them, in charitable deeds and in penances practiced for their sakes.

This belief in a hereafter explains the remarkable educational force, the almost incredible source of energy, that emanates from a parent's grave and affects their surviving children. Life shows surprising cases of children, whose conduct often grieved their parents, becoming serious and quite changed at the parent's grave.

D. The warmth of this belief in a hereafter stirs up, in the hearts of parents mourning for their dead children, manifestations of charity toward their fellow men.

1) The moment when parents stand beside the coffin of one of their children, is a touchingly painful one. The mail has brought me sad letters from many a heartbroken mother who has seen her lovely young daughter or her only son laid in the grave. After that the bereaved mother sits staring before her in silent despair with dry eyes, or with her faith in divine goodness shaken, struggling alone without any consolation.

2) What shall I say to such a one? What can give her consolation? Nothing but the sunbeam shining upon us from the next world.

The bereaved mother who believes in that next world does not bury in her child's grave the most beautiful ornament of a woman's soul, maternal love, but pours out this love upon other children who have become orphaned, or expends it upon those who have never known a parent's love.

I know of a mother who remained in desolate despair after the death of her child, until someone advised her to begin knitting socks and making little shirts for children just the size of her own little son, no longer for her own child but for little sufferers. And then, as the product of her knitting-needles increased, the anguish of grief decreased in her heart. Perhaps her little son sent her this sunbeam from the other world.

II

LIFE'S HARDSHIPS

In the sunlight of that other world I have a different view of life's hardships.

A. The perfect dispensation of justice in the hereafter is a consolation in bitter moments of earthly injustice. Our grief at unjust neglect or unfair judgment is gently appeased by the perfect justice of the next world. We are saddened by death's inexorable dominion, its face has many solacing features. If we think life is unfair or that happiness has been meted out with false measures, let us go to the cemetery and there we shall be reconciled with our lot.

By the sunlight of the other world, we see that all earthly life is like a great game of chess. While the game continues, there are kings and queens, knights and peasants. But when the game is at an end, all alike are swept from the board and each one comes into the silent box, into his coffin; no longer is there king and peasant, and knight. There is only one: the soul freed from the body, and according to the way it has obeyed God's commandments and performed the duties of earthly life, it awaits its sentence from divine justice. And then comes true a little German rhyme that we may render thus:

> As we believe, so do we live;
> And as we live, so shall we die;
> And as we die, so we remain.

B. By this light from the other world, Christianity offers the most optimistic view of life, because this religion gives strength to bear the hardest fate.

1) When relentless death yearly mows down millions around us, so that the idea might easily come into our minds that man lives only to die, Christianity is able to chant the triumph of eternal life.

From the moment of his birth every man wrestles with death. A man hastens from one piece of work to the next; another man from pleasure to pleasure. One wakens from a wretched night to another wretched day; the other from a night spent in dancing to a day of gaiety. Each is on his way toward death.

But Christ is a greater lord than death; therefore He gives strength for the most difficult life. You have lost all your property? Your small capital is exhausted? Everyone who loved you has died? Your life is bitter? You are disappointed?

If you were richer than even the richest millionaire, of what advantage would that be to you when you must leave this life? And if you have been poorer than poor Lazarus and suffered more than the holy Job, but you have lived according to God's will, what an asset this will become in the next world!

2) The belief in a world to come always was and is a marvelous source of strength in moments of calamity. On March 26, 1827, one of the world's greatest musicians died; musical eras are reckoned from his third symphony as history is reckoned from the birth of Christ. And at the zenith of his career, this Beethoven became deaf. In 1822 he wished to conduct the only opera he composed, "Fidelio." At the rehearsal, singers and orchestra are thrown into confusion. They begin again. Again all is confusion. The dreadful truth flashes upon the great composer: I have become deaf!

Could a more appalling disaster have befallen him? And how did he behave in the face of it? Did he collapse? Did he take poison? Did he shoot himself? No. "I grasp fate by the throat," he writes. Whence came his superhuman strength? From the sunbeam that shone upon him from the other world, from his belief in life everlasting.

3) But perhaps I should not mention such remote examples. Shall I mention some modern ones, too?

Then see, two letters. Not an imaginary philosophy, not an improvised instance, but two letters that were really written. And what is related in them really happened recently to two sisters.

The mother of Margaret and Mary, two warm-hearted, deeply sensitive sisters, died. Life then swept the sisters far apart. Here are two letters that they wrote to each other. I repeat: these letters were really written by them; I did not compose them.

Here is the first one:

October 25, 1925.

My dearest Mary:

Eugene and I have just returned home from the cemetery, where we took two large pots of magnificent flowering white chyrsanthemums to dear mother's grave in our own name and yours, the best we in our poverty could afford. We also took two large bouquets of fir-branches. You can light a little candle at home, or look at those wonderful perpetual tapers, the stars—if the skies are not cloudy—and pray for her and Daddy and Augustus . . . and for all the other good souls who have gone on before to the eternal home.

Where shall we be a hundred years hence?

I might well have said less than a hundred years. By then new faces, new figures will walk the face of the earth, only here and there some feature or some movement will be a reminder that they were the little children playing around us today. A drop of our blood, a little trace of our souls, may still be found somewhere.

Humanity now seems strangely to resemble a great uniform river, the past, the present, and the future, flowing from one infinity to the other, its way leading for a little space through the educational province of "earthly life." There is a "next world," but it is so very different that we can have no idea of it. How can a root or a seed in the damp, dark earth imagine an entirely different world where there is light and air and warmth, and where it will bloom in indescribable delicacy of tint and fragrance? And where it will be able to create. You know that is what I should love to know and to do in eternity. I do not want "eternal rest," but eternal activity. To be at rest, yes, at rest that I am on the right path, that I cling to the dear Lord, and He will not forsake me. But otherwise I should like to help Him, and on my memorial cards, besides perpetual light, wish me good work too! And do not cut flowers for my grave, but pray for me and have mass said for the salvation of my soul.

But how far I have wandered from what I began to say! In a word, your flowers are also lying on dead Mama's grave. But do not think of her grave if you want to meet her. Let us seek her where there is no death, that is, with the dear God. This is not a place, this heaven, it is the continuation of the life of spiritual qualities, of goodness of a dear and beautiful individuality in another sphere, in timeless and spaceless dimensions. Let us be worthy of her memory by our patience, by the calmness with which we bear our troubles, in forgiveness, in love. This mortal existence passes so quickly; in a happier, spiritualized form, not subject to bodily illnesses, we shall all meet again.

That is the end of the one letter.

I will read a few lines of the sister's reply:

Transientness, transientness. Either sooner or later everything passes, everything, whether it is good or whether it is painful. The children grow up, we slowly disappear, then they quietly grow old and their children too, and a strange spirit of the times, a strange era will come. It is not worth while making a great fuss about our lives, our well-being, our belongings. They will not last forever, we cannot take them with us. . . . Why cling to things

from which our hands slip, or which slip from our hands. We
need something absolute, something changeless, and eternally ideal
and calm.

I "died" long ago, in the sense that I have laid my old standards,
ambitions, fancies, longings, and demands at the feet of Him
who gave me life and who can take back my life at any moment.
And I have "risen again" to the fulfilment of my duties and only
beg that I may be allowed to bring up my children, that I may
harm no one, and may always know what is demanded of me by
circumstances, and that I may always stand fast to my principles.
We can never know what is good and what is bad for the develop-
ment of our "permanent part," and rather shall the children grow
up in poverty to love of work, to commonsense views of life, than
in prosperity to self love, and a desire for comfort and pleasure.
In this way I take what comes with great inward tranquillity and
am exceptionally grateful for every little joy. And the result is
that I am much, much happier than when I wanted to have my
own way or when I wanted to dictate to God how He should
order my destiny, that He should help me, but at once. And how
and in what manner He should help. Curing my bronchial catarrh,
He sent me a digestive complaint. That I should paint. He sent
poverty so that I had to earn money. With this period of house-
work perhaps He will heal my stomach complaint, or it will have
some effect on the children's future. But it is certain that in everything He gives some positive good.

That is the second letter.

Shall I add anything to it, my dear brethren? Shall I draw
attention to the fine, spiritual tranquillity that is brought to
suffering hearts by the sunbeam from the other world? Shall
I say that they do not fear to look to the world beyond the
grave, whose graves are surmounted by the cross of Christ?

The great Apostle of the Gentiles, St. Paul, in his epistle
to the Romans, speaks fifty-seven times of the dreadful reality
of death; yet he is able to say these beautiful words of spir-

itual reassurance: "None of us liveth to himself, and no man dieth to himself. For whether we live, we live unto the Lord; or whether we die, we die unto the Lord. Therefore whether we live or whether we die, we are the Lord's" (Rom. 14: 7, 8). Amen.

XII

DEATH THE COMFORTER

A⊤ the entrance to old Italian cemeteries we often find two interesting statues. One represents sorrow: it is the statue of an afflicted man bent by grief, with an extinguished torch at his feet; the other is the personification of life eternal, of resurrection, of renewed meeting: it is the statue of a handsome youth, a star glistens on his forehead, and his shining eyes look upward.

These two statues are well placed at the entrance to a cemetery; for death has indeed such a twofold figure. The one is a rattling skeleton with a sharp scythe in its hand, and wherever it appears the bitter weeping of mourners breaks forth. Its voice at such a time is the mysterious voice heard by the great prophet Isaias of the Old Testament on one occasion: "The voice of one saying: Cry! And I said: What shall I cry? All flesh is grass and all the glory thereof as the flower of the field. The grass is withered and the flower is fallen" (Is. 40: 6, 7).

Yes, all life is as grass. This is one representation of death: a rattling skeleton.

But there is another representation of death, and to me this seems much more the Christian idea: when death is depicted as an angel. The angel of death. His voice is the consoling voice that the Apostle St. John heard: "Write: Blessed are the dead who die in the Lord" (Apoc. 14: 13). This voice is the voice of eternity.

Eternity. St. Augustine calls it *magna cogitatio,* "the great thought." After all, this is the only truly great thought, strong and imparting strength, a thought reassuring and encouraging. Other human thoughts are concerned only with earthly life and come to an end with earthly life: but this thought speaks most beautifully in death's realm, in the land of graves. It goes to every mourner, to every orphaned heart, to everyone struggling with sorrow, and repeats Isaias' question: "Knowest thou not or hast thou not heard? The Lord is the everlasting God. . . . They that hope in the Lord shall renew their strength, they shall take wings as eagles, they shall run and not be weary, they shall walk and not faint" (Is. 40: 28, 31).

What can make death, appalling and dreadful death, bearable, a solacing, encouraging angel? These two thoughts: death is the end of earthly life; death is the beginning of life everlasting.

I

THE END OF EARTHLY LIFE

The first consolation given by the angel is that death puts an end to earthly life and to all the suffering and injustice that is entailed by life.

A. Death puts an end to all earthly suffering. I scarcely need to say much about this. These words of Holy Writ require no explanation: "O death, thy sentence is welcome to the man that is in need, and to him whose strength faileth; who is in a decrepit age and that is in care about all things" (Ecclus. 41: 3, 4). And St. Ambrose declared: "Life is full of so much trouble that death, compared to it, seems rather to be a remedy than a penalty."

How much suffering accompanies man on his earthly pilgrimage! How much pain, how many tears! And in life
everlasting all this is at an end. "They shall no more hunger
nor thirst, neither shall the sun fall on them, nor any heat,
for the Lamb, which is in the midst of the throne, shall rule
them and shall lead them to the fountains of the waters of
life, and God shall wipe away all tears from their eyes"
(Apoc. 7: 16, 17).

Is it any wonder that many invalids greet death joyfully
when he steps to their bedside with the sand run down in the
hourglass in his hand and whispers into their ear the Lord's
message: "The time has come when you may rest from your
labors" (Apoc. 14: 13). Death is a cessation from all suffering.

B. Furthermore, death is a dispenser of justice. This earthly
life abounds in so much injustice; so many times evil con-
quers, and honor suffers defeat. Thereby many are often very
embittered. But when we are severely tormented by the many
injustices of earthly life, let us go to the cemetery among the
quiet dead, and there our rebellious hearts will become
calmer. Death is a dispenser of justice. Rank and position
count for nothing in his eyes, he cannot be bribed with wealth,
nor cajoled with smiles; he accepts no one's recommendation
of another.

Perhaps you know the German ballad of the bells of Speyer.
A poor man died, says the ballad, and in the tower the big
emperor-bell pealed forth, the bell that usually tolled only
when an emperor died. And the populace said: "The emperor has died, the emperor has died." Later emperor Henry
V really did die, but when only a little passing-bell tolled,
and people asked one another: "Who can the poor sinner be
who today has come to judgment?"

I am sure you feel the symbolism of this ballad: that death

is a dispenser of justice. In his realm every earthly difference disappears, and every true difference, every spiritual value, appears.

C. Thus death equalizes the social inequalities of earthly life. "Give an account of thy stewardship" (Luke 16: 2). You stand before a Judge who cannot be bribed. Whether you were renowned or unknown, wealthy or poor, the scion of an old family or of an obscure one, emperor or beggar, these differences are now of no account. "For we brought nothing into this world, and certainly we can carry nothing out" (I Tim. 6: 7).

Some may recall the profound symbolism of the burial in the crypt of the Vienna Capuchins of the mighty ruler Francis Joseph I in the year 1916.

The lord steward of the royal household knocks at the door of the crypt.

"Who asks for admittance?" is the question put from the depths of a vault by a Capuchin father.

"The emperor and king, Francis Joseph I," answers the lord steward.

"I do not know him."

The lord steward again knocks at the door.

"Who asks for admittance?"

"Francis Joseph of Habsburg."

"I do not know him," is again the reply.

The knocking is repeated for the third time.

"Who asks for admittance?"

"A poor dead person."

At that the door of the crypt is opened and the coffin admitted.

In death all earthly distinctions disappear, but all true distinctions become important.

D. Death sometimes cancels our debts to God. Death and

its precursor, suffering, may be a sinner's opportunity to atone for his sins. Who can say he has no atonement to make in the sight of God? Even if those sins have been confessed, has sufficient atonement been made?

In a beautiful, ennobling, and exalting prayer zealous Christians offer their deaths to God in humble surrender during their years of health and strength: "My Lord, whenever and wherever death overtakes me, under whatever circumstances, I accept it at Thy hand as expiation for my sins."

Thus St. Paul's words become true in us: "For to me . . . to die is gain." How could it be otherwise, when death puts an end to earthly suffering, dispenses justice, equalizes inequalities, and cancels our debts?

II

THE BEGINNING OF LIFE EVERLASTING

Death has a still more consoling, more encouraging feature. At the same time that death lifts the cross from our shoulders, our holy religion erects it on our graves as a sign of consolation. That cross proclaims that with death life everlasting begins and therefore death is a homecoming to our heavenly Father. This is what makes death a consoling angel.

A. Real life begins with death.

1) On every building the roof is important, that is, the conclusion of every work is important. The concluding words of the Creed are important. If there is no life everlasting, what is all the rest worth: of what value is God, Christ, the Church, the whole of life? If there is no eternal life, of what worth is this earthly life? It would be an aimless struggle.

On the other hand, if I am a Christian I believe in life everlasting. I believe that here on earth I have only a little piece of life in my hand; the greater part of it, the endless part, is in God's hand. And what is here obscure, uncertain, unjust, and anguishing is dispelled in that other part, and all becomes bright and glorious. Christianity displays profound psychology when it calls the day on which a saint has died *dies natalis,* his birthday. Death is not destruction, and man does not remain the grave's eternal prisoner.

Every grave will fare as one in Hannover fared. There in an old cemetery stands the grave of a distinguished woman who died in 1782. Her tombstone bears the following strange inscription: "This grave, bought for all time, must never be opened."

"For all time—never." What weighty words!

Yet the grave was opened; opened neither by an earthquake nor by human hands. At the foot of the tombstone a little birch tree began to grow. The little tree became a big tree and in time removed from its path everything that obstructed its growth. Iron clasps were bent, stones were moved from their places and now this mighty tree stands in the middle of the grave. It did not trouble much about "for all time" and "never." Thus in Joseph of Arimathea's garden our Lord opened the sepulcher that many wished to keep closed forever. Ever since then on our graves the cross of this risen Savior proclaims that the last word does not belong to death, but to life.

2) We know that death is the great sower, and the graveyard is God's acre. This is quite a biblical expression. You know Jesus' words: "Unless the grain of wheat falling into the ground die, itself remaineth alone; but if it die it bringeth forth much fruit" (John 12: 25). So according to our Lord we must die that we may live. That is why St. Paul declares that in baptism, we are baptized for death: "Know you not that all we who are baptized in Christ Jesus, are baptized in His death?" (Rom. 6: 3).

What things we often see on graves! What pagan representations! The most fitting ornament is the cross. The cross with this inscription: "I believe in life everlasting." I believe that what we call death is a transition from one form of life to another. Transition to that other life, where the heavenly Father awaits us.

Can there be anyone who does not believe this? Our Lord spoke of it again and again. There mourners shall be comforted, there the pure of heart shall see God (Matt., chap. 5). There will be held the marriage feast where we must appear in wedding garments (Matt. 22: 12). There the good fish will be separated from the bad fish (Matt. 13: 48). There is the house mentioned by Christ: "In My Father's house there are many mansions" (John 14: 2). At death the true, the higher life begins.

3) What will our death be like? No one can tell. But I imagine that all at once the room will grow dark where I lie on my sickbed. The electric light will burn in vain, I no longer see it. I am already feeling my way along a corridor. But that does not last very long. All at once at the end of the corridor a door opens wide and I stand in a dazzling flood of light in the next world. The doctor has hardly said "He is dead"; but my soul already stands in the radiance of perpetual light. Have you ever seen the wide-open eyes of a little child when its mother first takes it into the candle-lighted room on Christmas Eve, where "little Jesus" has already been? Well, so we too shall stand when, after our long pilgrimage, we return home, from this "vale of tears" to where "little Jesus" has not only "been" but where He lives eternally.

In truth he who thinks that death takes the members of his family to some immeasurable distance from him, does not think rightly of death. On the contrary, death abolishes all distance between us because it liberates the soul from every limitation imposed on it by matter. Death does not disperse a family; the deceased members of the family continue to belong in the midst of us; they are simply living in another home. Living there and waiting for us there.

Thus death's forbidding features become reassuring, consoling, encouraging. Death is indeed a great secret, a great mystery. *Mysterium iniquitatis,* the mystery of sin, because through sin and on account of sin death came into the world. But it is also *mysterium caritatis,* the mystery of love, because the despairing feature of our own death has already been taken away by another great death, our Lord's death of redemption.

Happy death? Is such a thing possible? Is it true that people have died smiling calmly, with a peaceful expression, with confident surrender to the divine will?

Did they not feel the pains of illness? Yes, but hope and the yearning for God was still stronger within them. Did they not regret leaving this earth? Yes, but their longing to possess heaven was still greater. Did they not know the fear of death? Yes, but their yearning for life everlasting conquered it. Did they not perceive the angel of death? Yes, but they also saw the consolation and beauty of his face.

The thought of such a "happy death" is the greatest consolation in the hour of our own death. An architect does not mourn when he has finished a building. An artist is not sad when he has put the last touches to a picture. A soldier at the end of a successful battle. The wanderer who has reached his goal. The mariner upon coming into port. A child is not sad when it comes home to its father.

B. In that thought we have discovered the most comforting feature of death's face. Death is a homecoming to our heavenly Father. "I leave the world and I go to the Father" (John 16: 28).

1) Says a French writer (Vinet): "The Christian is a man of desires." Certainly a holy homesickness draws us toward the eternal kingdom of our heavenly Father as rivulets are drawn toward the great ocean, as a wanderer is drawn toward his home, as the magnet is attracted by the magnetic pole. We are never satisfied with today, but await what the morrow will bring. Never was the past year good enough, we always wish for a happier new year. Because we all feel that "we have not here a lasting city, but we seek one that is to come" (Heb. 13: 14).

This longing made St. Paul say that he had a desire "to be dissolved and to be with Christ" (Phil. 1: 23). Death is the great dissolution, the unveiling of the soul: then the material partition wall falls, the wall that hid God's face from our sight.

Death is the gratification of the portentous longing that makes man a restless sojourner here on earth. "While we are in the body, we are absent from the Lord" (II Cor. 5: 6), is St. Paul's lament. Here we live, as it were, in a hotel room. Who would wish to settle down definitely in such a room?

The final object of all our fervent longings is God, our final home is God's kingdom. The realm where the words of Holy Writ are realized: "Behold the tabernacle of God with men, and He will dwell with them and they shall be His people and God Himself with them shall be their God" (Apoc. 21: 3).

Now we understand why our hearts beat with joy when our Lord speaks of death as a homecoming to the Father (John 14: 2). Who would not be joyful when after a long sojourn abroad he at last returns home to his Father's house? When those who are weary and overburdened may lay aside their tools, their kitchen work, their pens; may throw the heavy knapsacks from their shoulders and rest in a place where "God shall wipe away all tears from their eyes, and death shall be no more, nor mourning, nor crying, nor sorrow shall be any more" (Apoc. 21: 4).

2) Death is also a day of compensation: the crowning of all our self-discipline, of our every battle, of all our renunciation.

When the abbot St. Hilary came to the end of a long disciplined and repentant life, and the fear of death tortured him greatly, he encouraged his departing soul in these words: "Step forth; what fearest thou? Break forth, my soul, why dost thou hesitate? For nearly seventy years thou hast served Christ; shalt thou now fear death?" What a consolation for anyone to be able to say this!

"O sweet brother death," cries St. Francis of Assisi in the "Hymn to the Sun," that he wrote before his death. Truly the death of the righteous is as tranquil and bright as a beautiful sunset. Above them hover the words of Holy Writ as the Church applies them: "Precious in the sight of the Lord is the death of His saints" (Ps. 115: 15).

3) It is true, nevertheless, that the thought of this homecoming is likewise a warning for us.

This question was once put to Epaminondas: "Whom dost thou consider the greatest, Chabrias, Iphicrates, or yourself?" To which Epaminondas replied modestly: "First see how we shall die; only then can one judge."

So it is, my brethren. How shall we die? Do you wish to know how we shall die? It is easy to reply to that. We shall die as we have lived. For Dante's words are true (*Inferno,* cant. 14, line 51): "What I was in life, I am in death." He who has cared for his soul, for eternal life, for God, while enjoying good health, will find God beside him when the great moment approaches. He will be able to look into death's eyes as St. Francis of Assisi did.

4) And in this we find death's final consolation. Now comes the grand "unveiling of the statue." Mortal life is no more than the scaffolding of a building in course of construction. If then the work of the soul is finished, the scaffolding is removed and the building appears.

Does everything pass, is everything engulfed by the shoreless ocean of time? Oh no. There is something that triumphantly defies time. And what is this? Every little stone that we built into our souls. Every little good intention, thought, word, and deed of ours derived from God. All our pain and suffering, all our unselfish love, all our patience and loyalty, every moral victory of ours; all this remains forever. It is true that in the same way our every weak moment and failure, our every infidelity and lack of principle, all our cowardice and falsity, all our dark hours and dark deeds remain too.

Thus we see the nature of our life's task: to build ourselves, to ennoble and beautify our souls, until the angel of death comes for us. This building work is the duty of each one in whatever position or under whatever circumstances he lives his life on earth. Whether our lifework is in the kitchen or in the factory, in the office or in the hospital ward, whatever it is in the world, this task awaits all of us: the building of our souls. Therein we find life in death; and he who finds life in death ceases to fear death.

"All flesh is grass," said the prophet Isaias. "The grass is withered and the flower is fallen" (Is. 40: 7). If that were all, it would be calamitous. But this truth has an exalting continuation: grass that is withered will grow again. This truth is dreadful only for those whose roots have broken away from God, from the life-giving soil of the soul. "For if you live according to the flesh, you shall die, but if by the Spirit you mortify the deeds of the flesh, you shall live" (Rom. 8: 13). "What things a man shall sow, those also shall he reap. For he that soweth in his flesh, of the flesh also shall reap corruption. But he that soweth in the spirit, of the spirit shall reap life everlasting" (Gal. 6: 8).

The wicked "shall shortly wither away as grass, and as the green herbs shall quickly fall" (Ps. 36: 2). But "the just shall flourish like the palm tree; he shall grow up like the cedar of Libanus" (Ps. 91: 13).

Then let us listen to death's last admonition: When you came into the world, you wept bitterly, but around you everyone rejoiced. So live that when you leave the world, even if everyone around you weeps, you will rejoice, rejoice in the eternal bliss that awaits you.

My dear brethren. Up two sides of Switzerland's famous mountain, the Rigi, climb cog-wheel railways. One of them starts at Vitznau on the shore of Lake Lucerne, the other at the foot of the other side of the mountain, at Goldau.

On the platform of the Goldau railway station a notice states that underneath the station nearly five hundred persons lie buried, together with the church and more than a hundred houses.

On September 2, 1806 there was a landslide down the side of the Rossberg, burying the five hundred inhabitants under a mass of rocks and earth. The rocky mass still lies in ominous proximity to the railway; beneath it an entire village lies buried.

There, too, lies the village church. On the day of the catastrophe, in the church, in the Holy Eucharist, the Lord Jesus Christ also descended into the underground grave.

What a consoling thought: Christ is also buried with His followers who died so suddenly. What a consoling thought! For to suffer is not the most dreadful thing; but to suffer without Christ. To be buried is not the most awful thing; but to be buried without the hope of resurrection.

Lord Jesus, help us Thy followers, that if we suffer in life our every suffering may be mitigated by our belief in life everlasting.

Lord Jesus, help us, Thy followers, that when we die we may be fortified in death by the consolation of our home-coming.

Lord Jesus, help us, Thy followers, that if we are buried we may before dying once more receive the Holy Eucharist and be buried together with Thee, that the hope which animated St. Paul may also animate us: "I have fought a good fight, I have finished my course, I have kept the faith. As to the rest there is laid up for me a crown of justice which the Lord, the just Judge, will render to me in that day" (II Tim. 4: 7, 8). Amen.

XIII

DEATH THE VANQUISHED

Wно has not heard of the cemetery at Pisa and the famous frescoes above its entrance? The largest painting, "The Triumph of Death," commemorates the dreadful plague of 1348. In this picture, life is represented by a pleasant green park; amid music, games, and pleasure, the people pass their days, but in the distance death is seen approaching on dark pinions, with fearfully flowing white hair. The people do not observe his approach, until all at once he smites with his scythe into the midst of the merrymakers. Certainly this "Triumph of Death" is a picture calculated to make everyone shudder.

But on a different part of the wall another picture is to be seen: tranquillizing, comforting. This is not death triumphant, but death vanquished. Here no flower-garden is symbolical of earthly life, but a somber valley surrounded by rocky crags, "the Vale of Tears." This, too, is full of people, just as the park in the other picture. They also die as do those others, but not with contorted faces. Each face expresses a holy longing, a sacred calm; each one yearningly stretches out his arms toward death: here death is not victorious, death has been overcome, vanquished.

Death vanquished? Is there such a thing? The most beautiful manifestation of belief in life everlasting is when mortal man overcomes death. Because death can triumph only over those who do not believe in life everlasting. This thought I intend to set forth in the first part of today's discourse; afterward to consider that he who believes in eternal life vanquishes death. Christ aids him to overcome it when He appears beside his sickbed.

I

THOSE WHO ARE VANQUISHED BY DEATH

A. What is man's life but a ceaseless struggle with death and a continual dread of death? We eat and drink, rest and amuse ourselves, recruit our strength and undergo medical treatment: all this is a forced concession, a brief respite extorted from death's niggardly hand.

When someone dies who is dear to us, we say while weeping bitterly: Life is so short! Does everything pass so quickly? Does everything perish?

Yes, dear brethren, everything perishes. "We belong to death, and everything that is ours is his," says the Latin poet. Horace.

> This world, this earthly life
> For young and old is only strife,
> First we laugh, then we sigh,
> And the end is that all must die.

How dreadful it must be when a person feels his strength decreasing, feels that death is approaching, and has nothing to say to him! Nothing but what the wretched Nietzsche said:

"The crows are cawing and wending their swift way toward the town. So it will snow; alas for him who has no home!"

Who is it that has no home when the freezing eventide of life comes? He who has no faith. Only such a man, an unbeliever, is vanquished by death.

B. However we patch and mend our lives, death seems to triumph after all. With a few skilful strokes of his pencil,

Dürer has shown us a startling picture of death: Death sits on a horse, emaciated to a skeleton, on his head a ghostly crown sparkles; in his outstretched hand is a scythe with which he mows down everything wherever he goes in this world. The title of the picture is, "King Death."

The picture is true, yet not true. It is true because there is no living thing on earth that can escape the power of death. But it is also not true, because there was Someone who was stronger than death on his galloping horse: Christ who overcame death, Christ the Lord of life. And everyone who clings to the hand of the Christ who vanquished death, is stronger than death.

An elderly physician once said: In my fifty years of medical practice I have seen thousands die. Some awaited death with a dull resignation reminiscent of the animals, some with impotent rage, some resisted despairingly and awaited its coming in fear and trembling. Only one kind awaited death calmly and peacefully: believing Catholics.

Is this true? Is it possible? Is it possible that one dies and at the same time overcomes death? What is the secret of this? What gives us, mortal men, strength to vanquish the dreadful tyranny of death?

II

THOSE WHO VANQUISH DEATH

A. The answer cannot be doubted: Whoever believes in life everlasting vanquishes death.

1) There is hardly anyone who does not know the first line of the Bible: "In the beginning God created the heavens and the earth" (Gen. 1:1). These are sublime words.

But if I were now to ask what are the very last words of the last book of Holy Writ, I am afraid few persons could tell me. Yet they are sublime, vivifying words.

"Come, Lord Jesus" (Apoc. 22: 20) says the Apostle St. John in the closing lines of the last book of the Bible, the Apocalypse. Holy Writ could not end with a more beautiful longing than this; and we cannot close our own life with a more beautiful desire.

2) What is life? Ceaseless fear of death. This fear weighs on our entire lives and enfeebles them. How much more a man's life would be if he did not fear death!

Those who are accustomed to consider earthly life from the standpoint of life everlasting, in their last moments will calmly listen to the consoling prayer of holy mother Church, which is said beside the dying by a priest: *Proficiscere, anima christiana,* "Set out on thy way, Christian soul."

Come, brethren, set out. Earthly life was the pilgrimage, now is the homecoming. Earthly life was the battle, now comes the victory. Earthly life was the test, now comes the reward. Earthly life was a voyage, now comes the harbor. Earthly life was the night, now comes the sunrise, the light eternal. *Proficiscere,* set out on thy way, Christian soul. For unbelievers death is a leap into darkness, an appalling leap. For the believer it is the gentle opening of a door.

If shortly before his death Socrates possessed sufficient spiritual strength to sacrifice a cock to the gods in gratitude because he was soon "to be cured of the illness, life," with much better reason we can look up hopefully toward the opening gates of our eternal home.

B. I look at the graves in our cemeteries and my eyes fasten their gaze on a great symbol: the cross erected upon the graves. On our graves the arms of the cross point heavenward and speak of a consoling truth: the grave is not the last word, the grave is incapable of covering life, with death life is merely changed, it is not lost. *Obdormivit in Domino* says the Church most consolingly of the dead, they "fell asleep in the Lord."

Let this falling asleep in the Lord come. What does it signify to one who has striven all his life to serve God? The end of a race, the crowning triumph of a struggle, the dying away of battle, the overcoming of death. For one who has overcome death, the solemn tolling of funeral bells proclaims the Easter of life eternal. To him funeral bells ring in the Sun, the Sun that has risen never more to set.

C. Whoever thinks in this way may indeed mourn for his loved ones, but his mourning will be of a different sort.

1) St. Paul counsels us not to mourn for our dead as the unbelievers do. "Be not sorrowful even as those who have no hope. For if we believe that Jesus died and rose again, even so them who have slept through Jesus will God bring with Him" (I Thess. 4: 12, 13).

But what does that mean? Are we not allowed to mourn, are we not allowed to shed tears? O yes. We may weep for our dear ones who have departed. Is there any picture dearer to us, more widely known, than the picture of the *Mater dolorosa,* Sorrowful Mother, mourning for her dead Son? And that marvelous woman, St. Elizabeth of Hungary, did she not burst into tears when the news of her husband's death was brought to her?

We, too, may mourn, but not in a pagan manner. Not as "those who have no hope," but as those who know that death was vanquished by Christ. As those whose ears have heard St. Paul's stirring words: "This corruptible must put on incorruption, and this moral must put on immortality. And when this mortal hath put on immortality, then shall come to pass the saying that is written: Death is swallowed up in victory. O death, where is thy victory? O death, where is thy sting?" (I Cor. 15: 53–55.)

2) We can overcome, because death has already been overcome by Christ. After Christ's advent people still die, it is true, just as they did before He came to earth. But since His coming we know clearly and certainly that even after burial our souls, destined to eternal life, remain.

But death is not now such a victorious tyrant as he was before Christ came, because today we know that he destroys in us nothing but what is transient. Today death seems not to be the same dreadful reaper he was long ago, because now we know that he takes us from darkness to light, from sickness to health, from thirst to the fountain-head, from space and time to an infinity that knows no limitations.

Death was vanquished by Christ when He proclaimed that it is only a transition to a new, more beautiful life. As in nature some species become extinct to make way for more perfect ones, so at the end of life we step out of our own narrow frames that we may step into God's infinity.

Death was vanquished by Christ when He proclaimed that the corruption of our bodies that arouses so much horror, is nothing but the removal of a barrier that prevents us from entering our real home.

Death was vanquished by Christ when He taught mankind to face death courageously. The multitude turn their backs upon death and strive to escape from him. Of course they do not succeed and so they become death's victims. For the more anyone tries to flee from death, the more helplessly he falls into death's hands.

What happens to him who looks death in the face with head erect? Of course he too meets death, but freely, consciously, in the strength of a great future hope, triumphantly. This mortal overcomes death, for in the last great moment, there beside him holding his hand, stands Christ; the Christ who triumphed over death.

III

CHRIST BESIDE THE DYING

Now we have arrived at the final source of our victory. In the decisive moments of our last conflict, Christ stands beside us. This, my brethren, is not a mere figure of speech, a mere rhetorical ornament.

A. When we come into this world, in the ceremonies of our baptism, our holy religion places a lighted candle in our hands and places a white robe of innocence on us. When we are preparing to depart this life, it again lights this candle, endeavors to robe our souls anew in the white sanctified garment of grace, and brings Christ to our sickbeds in the Holy Eucharist.

1) "Receive this white garment," says the officiating priest at baptism in the first hours of our life, "which mayest thou carry without stain before the judgment seat of our Lord Jesus Christ, that thou mayest have life everlasting." "Receive this burning light and keep thy baptism so as to be without blame; observe the commandments of God, that when our Lord shall come to His nuptials, thou mayest meet Him together with all the saints in the heavenly court and live forever and ever."

Now we prepare to stand before the judgment seat of God, now the "wedding hour" has come. As mother Church stood by us in the first hours of our lives, so now she takes her stand beside us in this last hour. Then a lighted candle was in our hand, the symbol of faith, as it is now also. Now she washes us clean by the power of the sacraments of penance, the Holy Eucharist, and extreme unction.

2) Death and holy communion. Death and the eternal memorial of Christ's death. Death and the Holy Eucharist. How greatly they belong together! The death of frail man and the eternal memory of Christ's death! We priests know to how many persons, grievously ill, the administration of the sacraments has brought relief. Nurses and doctors can testify to how many sick people the reconciliation to God has brought alleviation, when no narcotic in this world was able to relieve their pain. Every experienced priest can tell of many sick people who, after a good confession, received in holy communion the Redeemer whom they had lost in the noisy bustle of life. But this Redeemer never rested until He could whisper reassuringly into the ear of His strayed sheep undergoing the hard struggle of the death agony: "I am the bread of life. If any man eat of this bread, he shall live forever" (John 6: 48, 52).

This is the final triumph over death. When every false allurement of the world fades away, when at life's end, like the farewell rays of the setting sun, our childhood's faith again shines forth and, bathed in tears of repentance, man contentedly places his soul in the hands of his heavenly Father. How grateful we should be to our Lord that He Himself comes to strengthen us in the final struggle.

B. How grateful we must be also because He has given a special sacrament to be administered to the sick in the most difficult hour, in fateful hours. "Is any man sick among you?" writes the Apostle St. James. "Let him bring in the priests of the church and let them pray over him, anointing him with oil in the name of the Lord; and the prayer of faith shall save the sick man, and the Lord shall raise him up, and if he be in sins they shall be forgiven him" (James 5: 14, 15).

1) Do you understand, my brethren, what this sacrament is for? Is it to bring death to the sick? That is what some

people seem to think. Is it that those to whom it has been administered are dying in any event and can now be buried? Certainly not. Here in this church sits a dear listener of mine, a professor of medicine at the university who has attended my sermons for many years. Last spring he became seriously ill, sent for me at once, received extreme unction. And did he die of it? Today he is here again, praying here with us and listening to the word of the Lord.

When we speak of extreme unction we speak of a sublime thing: of the sanctification of death, of the grace of a good death. This is the real euthanasia, good dying, and not an overdose of injections to send a sick person to the next world in a stupor. "To die well" is the most difficult art in the world. Everyone dies, but everyone dies only once, and we must attain this one death rightly.

2) Who does not fear death? Everyone with a healthy nervous system fears it. But Christ's sacrament mitigates our fear and fortifies our dismayed hearts.

While we are healthy we perhaps do not grasp what a terrible burden it can be, a more torturing spiritual suffering than the illness, when a sick man remembers his unfulfilled duties, his unrepaired faults, his old sins. This dreadful sense of guilt may consume more of his vitality than the bodily illness itself.

The memory of sins committed by the eyes. The many frivolous, sinful glances, for which it will be so difficult to account. But see, here beside us stands Christ's priest. Anointing our eyes with holy oil, he prays: "Through this holy unction and through His most tender mercy, may the Lord pardon thee whatever sins thou hast committed by seeing."

Again: how much improper, even sinful, conversation, how many indecent words, how much gossip, abuse, and unkind criticism! But see, now Christ's priest anoints our lips and prays: "Through this holy unction and through His most tender mercy may the Lord pardon thee whatever sins thou hast committed by taste and speech."

And he anoints our ears praying that God's mercy may pardon the sins we have committed by hearing—all of them, all of them.

And he anoints our hands that God's mercy may pardon the sins we have committed by touching—all of them, every one of them.

And he anoints our feet, that God's mercy may pardon the sins we have committed by walking—all of them.

This is real euthanasia, this is the art of a good death, this is victory over death, when, after receiving the sacraments, we can say with peace in our heart: Now I lay down my life in God's hands.

C. Dear brethren, is it not a heartless stupidity to deprive a sick person of this fortifying sacrament? Is it not an immense responsibility to postpone calling a confessor: No, not today. Tomorrow, sometime later. All at once comes sudden death; and the poor sick person, without having received the sacraments, goes to meet his God.

1) For a good death, strength is necessary; this strength can be given only by the grace of God. The more this world, with all its perfidious promises, disappears from the sight of the sufferer, the more intense the anxiety felt because of the approaching judgment, the more does he need the help of God's grace. Like a child who in a disturbing dream instinctively seeks its mother's helping hand, so a sufferer needs God's tranquillizing aid. I have never heard that the reception of the sacraments has harmed anyone, but I have often heard how greatly sufferers have been calmed and comforted after receiving them.

The wife of a dying man asked the physician this question: "Please tell me, doctor, shall I call a priest to my husband now, or will it be better to wait until he loses consciousness?" The doctor answered: "It depends, madam, whether you wish to help the sufferer, or merely wish to print on the mourning-cards that "the deceased passed on after devoutly receiving extreme unction."

2) What comedies—allow me to use this strong word—what comedies are often played in a sickroom! The sufferer would like to have the sacraments because he feels that nothing else can help his restless soul, but he hesitates to ask for a priest lest his relatives be alarmed. His relatives would be very glad if the sufferer were to receive the sacraments, but they hesitate to call a priest lest the sick man be alarmed. Meanwhile the sufferer becomes weaker and feebler: he loses consciousness and finally dies without Christ having come to his bedside to help him with His sacraments to vanquish death. And all this because of the relatives' sentimental, stupid, unchristian anxiety.

How much more earnest, more profound, more Christian, and more genuinely loving was the manner of thinking of a young married couple who promised each other on their wedding-day, that if either of them should become seriously ill at any time, the other would not fail to say: "My dear, the time has come." The time has come for you to ask Christ to be beside you. O yes, I believe that death does not gain the victory over such as these, but they vanquish death, for to their bedside comes the Christ who vanquished death. Above such a deathbed will radiate St. Paul's assurance: "If we believe that Jesus died and rose again, even so them who have slept through Jesus, will God bring with Him" (1 Thess. 4: 3).

My dear brethren. In Deuteronomy is described the death of the great leader of the Hebrew people. Sublime are the simple words in which Holy Writ speaks of the death of Moses. Moses went up to mount Nebo where the Lord showed him the Promised Land, the final earthly goal of his life's work. "And," says Holy Writ, "Moses, the servant of the Lord, died there in the land of Moab, by the commandment of the Lord, and He buried him (Deut. 34: 5).

What beautiful words! Moses arrives at the end, ordained by God, of his toilsome life. At the Lord's word, he lays his weary head upon His breast, as a tired child rests in its mother's arms. "And He buried him."

My Lord, such a calm, quiet passing grant to me also. That when the angel of death knocks at my door, I may fall asleep in Jesus and, cleansed in the last confession, united with Christ in the last communion, strengthened by extreme unction, I may confide my soul to Thy fatherly hands. Amen.

XIV

PURGATORY

WITH death, life is not finally at an end. On the contrary then real life begins, life that never ends. Death is not the last word in man's life: it is a gate through which we must pass to attain to a more glorious, more complete life.

Death is not the end of everything; rather everything then begins: an eternally happy life begins in God's kingdom if we have merited it by our earthly lives. Or an eternally painful life begins in the realm of perdition if we passed through the gate of death with our souls turned from God, crippled by a heavy burden of sin.

Besides these two alternatives of life hereafter, our holy religion speaks of a temporary form of life in the hereafter, life in purgatory. That is where sins repented and confessed, but not yet completely atoned for, must receive temporary punishment, that after the penance has been endured, we may enter into eternal bliss completely cleansed and purified.

Belief in purgatory is so consoling and reassuring, originating as it does in the innermost depths of the human heart, that we should feel a painful void in the structure of our religious system, if this doctrine were missing from it.

What would become of us if there were only heaven and hell? Who has the audacity to say of himself at the end of his earthly life, a life perhaps full of moral frailty, that his soul is not bound to make any reparation to offended divine justice? Who can believe that his soul is so pure and faultless that at the moment of death it can enter immediately into God's kingdom? The kingdom of that God before whose holiness even the angels veil their faces, for it is written of Him that "in His angels He found wickedness" (Job. 4: 18).

Indeed if there were no purgatory we should all have cause to despair, we who are not so good that after death we could enter heaven at once, nor, let us humbly hope, so wicked as to deserve damnation. That is why I devote the present sermon to the consideration of these important questions: Does purgatory exist? Of what does purgatory consist? What is correlative to the existence of purgatory?

I

THE EXISTENCE OF PURGATORY

According to the teaching of holy Church, there is a place for the souls of the dead where reassuring hope and tormenting pain are equally at home; there is a place where the souls of the dead suffer, but they suffer in the certain hope that their sufferings will come to an end. This place is purgatory.

A. The Catholic Church has proclaimed this belief since early times, Holy Writ and sacred tradition both declare it.

1) The existence of purgatory is attested by Holy Writ. In the Books of Machabees, that is, in the last books of the Old Testament, we read that Judas Machabeus "sent twelve thousand drachmas of silver to Jerusalem for sacrifice to be offered for the sins of the dead" (II Mach. 12: 43). "It is therefore a holy and wholesome thought to pray for the dead, that they may be loosed from sins" (II Mach. 12: 46). Thus we see that the Old Testament testifies to a belief that there is a place where penance may be done and forgiveness of sins be gained after death; and that the living may pray and offer sacrifices for these penitents.

In one place our Lord speaks of sins that will be forgiven "neither in this world nor in the world to come" (Matt. 12: 32). In speaking thus, He evidently teaches that there is a place after death where certain sins are forgiven.

Moreover St. Paul speaks plainly of purgatory. According to him, besides those who enter heaven immediately after death, are some whose earthly work "the fire shall try" (I Cor. 3: 13) and, if their work is found worthy, they too will be saved "yet so as by fire" (I Cor. 3: 15).

2) We find also that Christian tradition is unanimous in professing belief in the existence of purgatory.

In the earliest ceremonies of the celebration of mass, a distinguished place is occupied by the "commemoration of the dead." But without belief in purgatory, without the possibility of a purification of the souls of the dead, this commemoration would have no meaning at all.

Neither would the countless epitaphs on the early tombs in the catacombs; therein prayers are asked for the dead. "Pray for me." But for whom are we to pray? We cannot pray for those in hell, and there is no need to pray for those in heaven. Therefore only purgatory remains. Without belief in purgatory there would be no reason for all the many prayers and masses for the souls of deceased persons in which the surviving relatives and friends turn to God. Yet as early as the second century, Tertullian mentions that on the anniversary of the deaths of Christians their relatives were in the habit of having mass offered for the peace of their souls. Certainly those who are acquainted with the various epitaphs in the catacombs, the supplications, requests, and prayers, will not doubt that the earliest Christians were convinced that the living can be of help to the souls of the dead; in other words, that there is a purgatory.

B. Belief in purgatory is also a general conviction deeply rooted in the human soul. Therefore we find it in some form even in pre-Christian times, in pagan religions.

1) Different books of pagan ceremonies have come down to us, for example, books of Egyptian burial ceremonies, and these speak of propitiatory sufferings that must be endured by good souls that they may gain admittance to Osiris' heavenly kingdom. According to the Persians, the souls of the dead first had to make a weary journey through the twelve constellations of the Zodiac; only after that could they attain bliss. The Greek Stoics speak directly of the fire regions, where souls are purified of their faults. There is scarcely any pagan liturgy without prayers and sacrifices for the souls "wandering in shadows." We can truly say that some form of belief in purgatorial fire was mankind's common treasure long before Christianity. This shows how surely it originates in the noblest yearnings of the human soul and how greatly it satisfies its deepest cravings.

2) We know that even those who avowedly and theoretically have eliminated this doctrine from their articles of faith, do in reality still acknowledge it. For they too pray for their dead and practice almsdeeds in their name and for their sake; but this has no meaning unless there is the possibility of purification, unless purgatory exists.

Human reason itself leads us to the conclusion that for those who do not die in mortal sin, that is, for those who die in the state of grace, there must be a transitory place for atonement, for purification. Perpetrated crime requires punishment here on earth; for offense against God's laws satisfaction must be given. True, God is merciful; but His mercy does not make Him ignore and overlook it. That mercy is shown by His giving the possibility of atonement. And if we have not taken sufficient advantage on earth of this possibility by our practice of penance, compulsory penance and painful reparation await us in purgatory.

II

THE NATURE OF PURGATORY

A. Purgatory, as its name indicates, is a place of purification and expiation.

1) At the moment of judgment, God shows the soul what it should have been according to His eternal plan, and how far it is from this in reality.

If a person has died in the state of grace, but burdened by many faults and imperfections, his soul will, at the judgment, of its own accord declare: Lord God, with so many imperfections I cannot enter Thy kingdom. With such blemishes I could not live eternally in that realm whereof it is written: "The glory of God hath enlightened it, and the Lamb is the lamp thereof" (Apoc. 21: 23).

2) This imperfection will be felt by man before God's judgment seat. How should he not feel it when even here on earth all sensitive souls feel it? What does such a soul feel? It feels that we never finished with ourselves. We are never finished with ourselves, our own souls, our own spirituality. Who could, for instance, here on earth attain the full accomplishment of God's will, that we "be made conformable to the image of His Son" (Rom. 8: 29).

Nor are we ever finished with our work. The artist can never say that he is finished, nor can the teacher, the student, or the writer.

Purgatory will be the place where everything is rightly completed. There we shall receive what is still lacking to God's likeness in our souls. Purgatory will be the place where we shall place the keystone to the building upon which we have worked all our earthly lives. Purgatory will be the place of great restoration: there we shall correct the disfigurement and cover the scars that have marred our souls through sin on earth. As soon as this image of God becomes radiantly clear, our purgatory will be ended. We may then enter into God's eternal bliss.

B. If we thus grasp the purpose of purgatory, then we see how superficial is the view of those persons who consider the penance of purgatory as unworthy of God. "God should mercifully remit both sin and punishment," they say. "This is worthy of His beneficence. But not expiation and reparation."

1) What a shallow way of thinking! Whoever thoroughly reflects upon God's sublimity knows that man's rebellion against God, if it remained unpunished, could not be reconciled with God's infinite justice and with the majesty of the eternal moral order.

Sin, an offense against God, is taken lightly by the world today. Look about you and you will see with what incredible recklessness, with what revolting cynicism, sin is propagated among men. Where will everyone acknowledge the truth of the psalmist's words: "Thou art just, O Lord, and Thy judgment is right" (Ps. 118: 137)? Where will Christ's words become true: "Amen I say to thee, thou shalt not go out from thence till thou repay the last farthing" (Matt. 5: 26)?

God's two apparently conflicting attributes, His justice and His mercy, are brought into harmony by our belief in purgatory. According to this doctrine, justice demands the penalty, but mercy allows that this penance be mitigated, and abridged by loving solicitude of the living.

2) Thus also we understand the twofold character of purgatory: it is pain, but at the same time it is hope.

In what does the suffering of purgatory consist? It is the same as that of hell, except that it is not eternal.

Hence one punishment there is an unavailing yearning for God. Now we see who God is. Now our souls divested of their bodies would strive toward God, but they are impeded by sin not yet expiated. And besides this yearning, a real pain torments us that is greater than the most torturing pain of earthly life. This is one of the constituent elements of purgatory: a sorrowful atmosphere.

However, although this place is the scene of great suffering, it is not hell, nor is it the vestibule to hell; it is the vestibule to heaven. Those who are here are not in the devil's hand, but in God's hand, that is, they are in a state of grace. Furthermore, they possess the certain knowledge that this state of grace is no longer in peril, that they can no longer lose what we living people unfortunately can lose at any time. They, therefore, are already sure of their salvation. This is purgatory's other feature: hopeful and confident expectation.

Then what is purgatory? A joyous hell, a sad heaven. There souls rejoice because they are sure that they will some day enjoy God; but they also suffer because they cannot yet enjoy God. As surely as heaven is made heaven by the possession of God, and as surely as hell is made hell by the loss of God, so purgatory is made purgatory by this transitory character: transition between the future possession of God and the present loss of Him.

III

COROLLARIES TO THE DOCTRINE OF PURGATORY

I fear, dear brethren, that what I have just said was an unknown idea to some of you. We so seldom speak of purgatory and so seldom think of it. Yet splendid teachings and admonitions are latent in this article of our faith.

A. I will point out one or two of the corollaries to the doctrine of purgatory.

1) Belief in purgatory removes hell further from us. Christianity does indeed teach the shattering postulate that not only eternal bliss exists but also everlasting perdition.

How many persons are terrified and made despairing, yes, even brought to denial of faith, by the thought of an eternal hell. "Can God really be good, can He really be merciful, if He was capable of creating an eternal hell?" we hear them ask. This is perhaps the most difficult article of our faith to understand. But it immediately becomes more intelligible, more bearable, if we know that there is also purgatory, that there is opportunity to atone for the greatest sins repented and confessed.

The thought of hell might indeed be unbearable if there were no purgatory. Massillon, Louis XIV's orator, in the course of a sermon in St. Eustace's Church in Paris, said that the majority of people are damned. At the end of the sermon the congregation sprang up from their seats, terrified and despairing. The greater number of people are lost? Dreadful! An unbearable thought! And they were right. The preacher would have been right only if there were no purgatory.

2) Belief in purgatory brings heaven nearer to us. Some people are made faint-hearted by the high standard of heaven. "How far it is from us! How hard to attain! How can we satisfy such strict requirements?" But see how much nearer heaven is brought to us, how much easier its attainment is made, by belief in purgatory.

The picture we have formed of God's mercy gains its final decisive touches from it, since God is not only benign as heaven proclaims, not only just as hell attests, but also merciful, as is evidenced by purgatory.

Purgatory is an answer to those who charge our moral doctrine with excessive severity, saying that "it does not yield an iota of its principles," that "it does not reckon with human frailty," that "it demands so much that weak, sinful man cannot fulfil it even with the best will in the world."

Here is the answer. From our moral ideals, certainly nothing can be withdrawn. But if someone has become a victim of the imperfections of human nature in spite of his habitual good dispositions, then for him there always remains purgatory as a side-door to heaven. It is not the great portal but, after all, it is a door to heaven.

3) Purgatory is also the best answer to the false doctrine of reincarnation.

How admirably the Church feels the most deeply hidden longings of the human soul! Who would not long for a place of purification? Is this not the greatest consolation for everyone who honestly strives to do God's will, who wants to be good, pure, and faithful, but who time and again is brought to a fall by sinfully inclined human nature? What a consolation it will be for us if, before God's judgment seat, we can say: "It is true, dear Lord, that I was not good enough to be found worthy to enter heaven at once. But, thanks to Thy grace, neither was I wicked enough to be cast into hell. First sift me, cleanse me, as wheat is cleansed from chaff; and then receive me into Thy eternal kingdom."

Christianity proclaimed the reality of this "purifying suffering" long before obscure Eastern philosophies sowed the seed of erroneous beliefs in men's souls concerning reincarnation, beliefs that cannot be established by any argument whatever.

My brethren. You who perhaps coquet with the thought

of reincarnation, you who find it "so tranquillizing," "so comforting." You should know that we also believe in "a purification" after death. We also proclaim that every sin "must be expiated" and "must be atoned for." But for this we have no need of a doctrine of reincarnation teeming with contradictions and depriving earthly life of its seriousness, but we find the mute pain of quiet penance in purgatory amply sufficient.

Spiritualism, the invocation of spirits, reincarnation, and similar hazy, vacillating ideas, as substitutes for belief in purgatory, find a footing among those who lack the warmth of Catholic faith. This fact shows how suited to the human soul's yearnings is the belief in purgatory, and how impossible it is for us to endure the thought of being finally cut off from our dear dead, and how impossible it is to think we can no longer make them feel our love and gratitude after they have died.

B. Here, however, we have arrived at another thought: purgatory not only serves for our instruction, but also as a warning for us.

1) Purgatory enables our love to be stronger than death, to extend beyond the grave, purgatory makes it possible for us, living beings, to help the souls of those who have died.

Consoling is the Christian doctrine, that death cannot tear asunder the bonds of relationship and of friendship, that prayers said for them, mass offered for them, self-denial and good deeds practiced for them, can be of assistance to the dead and curtail their period of suffering.

A sad but real human trait is that many malign one another in life, embitter one another, quarrel, are ungrateful to their benefactors. Only when death has taken them from our midst do we awake to a late recognition of what a treasure we have lost. Often despairing mourners lament: "My mother has died, my wife, my brother, and I was so often unkind and heartless to them while they were alive. How sorry I am now! But what can I do, how can I make amends?"

How our holy faith consoles us with its teaching, that with our prayers and good deeds we can, at least now, after their death, discharge our neglected debt of gratitude, we can make amends for much of our heartlessness!

In this way developed the pious custom of zealous Christians to offer up prayers, almsdeeds, holy communion, and so on; they seek to shorten the time of penance for souls that are being purified.

We are always moved when we read the words in which St. Augustine refers to the death of his mother St. Monica. Augustine and his brother Navigius stand beside their dying mother. Navigius wishes that his mother could die on their native soil and not in a strange land. But the dying Monica says: "Bury my body wherever you please. Take no thought about that. Only one thing I beg of you: that at the Lord's altar, wherever you may be, remember me" (St. Augustine, *Confessions,* Bk. IX, chap. 11).

If only this were the first thing to occur to us in connection with our dead: to remember them at God's altar. How many flowers, how many wreaths are sent to funerals! This may be some consolation for the bereaved; the dead, however, do not profit by it in any way. But they do indeed profit by our prayers, the masses celebrated for them, and by our good deeds.

Monks of the Trappist Order, when they meet, greet one another with the words, *Memento mori,* "Remember death." Death is the end merely of earthly life; but it is not the end of love.

2) Belief in purgatory contains another warning for all

of us: to make as many amends as possible in this life for the
sins we have committed.

Man's life is filled with suffering, trouble, and sorrow, but
Christians see in these things the love of a merciful God. It is
the work of divine mercy that we are given opportunity to
do penance here on earth. Suffering comes to everyone. Hence
we are wise if we accept every bereavement, illness, privation,
the wicked treatment of men, every humiliation and difficult
task, with humble hearts: "Reckon this, my Lord, all this
patient endurance, as part of my amends."

Sorrow and suffering still remain, but the endurance of
them is easier and more meritorious.

My dear brethren. King Charles V of Spain, whom history
calls wise, once put a peculiar choice before his son. On one
table he placed a crown, on the other a sword; then he called
the boy and put the difficult question to him, which did he
wish to possess. The prince smilingly stretched out his hand
toward the sword and said: "By this I will deserve the other."

By the sword the crown. A truly Christian idea; in it is the
whole program of Christian spiritual life. By the sword the
crown. By the conquering of self, by courageous and determined battle against our evil inclinations, against exacting
instincts and temptations, to attain possession of eternal life.
True, in battle some wounds are received, in the conflict
failure threatens; but belief in purgatory bids us not to de-
spond.

This belief, although a serious doctrine, is also a joyous
one. It is a serious warning not to be contented and at peace
in our sins; but it is also a joyous solace, that we do not need
to despair because of our human weaknesses.

Days pass, the years are swallowed up, the shadow of the

grave lengthens, death and destruction terrify, but I bravely raise my head and cry out in their faces: No, no, you can do nothing to me. I am the son of Him whom you could not conquer: of Christ triumphant over death.

Clinging to the victorious Christ, I say daily: I believe in life everlasting. Here I am only a wanderer, my true home awaits me. Here I am only on a journey, God is at its end. Here I thirst for bliss, with God I arrive at the life-giving waters.

Lord God, we beg with confidence that some day we may arrive at this heavenly home and enter into Thy eternal realm: if not at once by the great shining gate of heaven—for that we are not worthy—at least through the side-door of purgatory. Amen.

XV

ETERNAL PERDITION

For sixteen years I have proclaimed God's word from this pulpit, but never have I faced such a difficult task as the one today. For sixteen years I have preached in this church to my attentive listeners, but never have I felt my duties as a herald of God's word to be so difficult and affecting as today, when I must speak of eternal perdition.

That heaven exists, this is easy to believe. That there is a place where all earthly suffering, pain, illness, and death ceases and where every moral exertion of ours receives its just reward. Yes, this we joyfully believe: heaven exists.

But does hell exist, too? Is the thought that God can punish eternally, not a mere figment of some imagination of the Middle Ages? That there does actually exist an eternity where (one begins to tremble at the very idea even) in never ending torment those sentenced to perdition live their eternal life!

"Why speak of this? It would be better never to utter the name of hell. Why frighten people with it? No one ever returned from hell. Who knows if it really exists?" Such objections are heard nowadays if anyone wishes to discuss this subject. Truly we do not speak of it from this pulpit in order to frighten, but with a serious object in view. "No one ever returned from the next world, so why speak of it?"

I wonder if anyone has ever returned from the sun? Or from the stars? Yet how much we know of the heavenly bodies and what a serious science the science of astronomy is!

Nor is it true that no one has ever come to us from the next world, because our Lord Himself came thence. What we know of the world to come we know from Him. From Him we know the two shattering truths of which I intend to speak today: Not only is there a heaven, but there is also a hell; and not only heaven lasts forever, but hell also. Surely two impressively serious doctrines: Hell exists and it is eternal.

I

HELL EXISTS

A. God's infinite sublimity and the gravity of God's commands demand a place where those who rebel against Him atone by suffering after death. This way of thinking is so suited to man's mentality that even without Christianity the reasoning human mind would have discovered it.

1) This truth was felt by religions that existed prior to Christianity. Appalling suffering has to be endured (according to the belief of the Greeks) by Tantalus, king of Phrygia, who killed his own son and prepared him for food. But in Hades, the place of perdition, Tantalus is tormented by eternal hunger and thirst as a punishment. Fruit and water stand in front of him, but when he stretches out his hand for them they recede from him. "The torments of Tantalus."

You have certainly heard of the Danaids, the forty-nine women who killed their husbands and now as a punishment must eternally fill a bottomless cask with water drawn in a sieve.

You have heard of Sysiphus, the cruel Corinthian ruler whose eternal punishment it is to roll a heavy stone uphill, and when he has almost reached the top, the stone rolls down. "The labor of Sysiphus."

You have heard of Ixion who is bound to a wheel in the depths of Tartarus and the wheel continually breaks his bones and never ceases to turn.

You have heard of Tytius whose heart is eaten piecemeal by ferocious vultures that are never satisfied.

You have heard of Theseus who sits eternally in the darkest depths.

Is it not strange that whereas many protest against the thought of damnation, longing to escape from the awful reality of hell, yet we always find the thought of eternal punishment in the religions of various peoples: the Indian Veda religion knows a hell just as does Buddhism, the religion of Zoroaster too, just as Mohammedanism.

We can truly say that belief in eternal perdition was the belief held by all mankind even before Christianity.

2) Reason itself leads us to this belief. That there really is a hell, that there must be a place where every sin receives its punishment, is a conclusion of even non-religious persons, because of the awful wickedness that exists in the world.

When on all sides we learn of the atrocities committed by men: of blood-curdling murders committed without a twinge of conscience, of robberies, of the widespread immorality, of truth and honor trampled under foot, who would not despair, who would not waver in his faith if there were no hell where all this dreadfulness will receive its well-deserved punishment?

That there is a place where, as our religion teaches, rebellious, fallen angels are punished, and that Satan is not a mythical personage invented to scare disobedient children, but is a sad reality, the frightful deluge of sin in modern life leads us to accept. For who understands the infernal wickedness, the abysmal corruption, the cunning godlessness, that we witness day by day on all sides, if we do not attribute it to the work of the devil, if it is not true that sometimes awful fires flame up from hell to scorch the earth?

B. The existence of what humanity presaged so strongly before the coming of Christ, was elevated to a certainty by the Christian religion.

It is true, brethren, that the dreadful thought of eternal damnation makes one shudder. I myself would be glad if I could honestly say: There is no hell; there is only heaven. But our holy religion declares this doctrine in so many forms that of its truth not the slightest doubt can remain.

1) You say there is no hell? But our Lord's precursor, St. John the Baptist, said that "every tree therefore that does not yield good fruit shall be cut down and cast into the fire" (Matt. 3: 10). And the same St. John the Baptist taught that at the judgment God will "gather His wheat into the barn, but the chaff He will burn with unquenchable fire" (Matt. 3: 12).

2) You say there is no hell? Then you give the lie to our Savior's plain and direct teaching. Again and again He spoke of hell.

No one can say that Christ wished to frighten people. But when He speaks of hell and of the torments of hell, His words are emphatic. Poor Lazarus came into the one eternity, the heartless rich man into the other; the five wise virgins came into the one, the five foolish into the other; of the good thief Christ said that the good thief would enter into His kingdom, into Paradise; speaking of Judas, our Lord said it would have been better for him had he never been born.

If hell is not the penalty for mortal sin, then there is no truth in Christ's words, when He said that it will profit a man nothing to gain the whole world if he suffers the loss of his soul (Matt. 16: 26).

You say there is no hell? But did not our Lord say that the wicked will come to a place "where their worm dieth not, and the fire is not extinguished" (Mark 9: 45)? And that same Christ who in the Sermon on the Mount spoke of the eight beatitudes, later spoke of "hell fire," too (Matt. 5: 22), where "there shall be weeping and gnashing of teeth" (Luke 13: 28). And that same Christ said: "Fear ye not them that kill the body, and are not able to kill the soul, but rather fear him that can destroy both soul and body in hell" (Matt. 10: 28). If there is no hell what does Christ mean by saying that at the judgment He will set some on His right hand, but some on His left? (Matt. 25: 33). And to the wicked He says: "Depart from Me, you cursed, into everlasting fire" (Matt. 25: 41); and then, "these shall go into everlasting punishment" (Matt. 25: 46).

3) You say there is no hell? But then you will have to reject what St. Paul declares. For he wrote: "We shall all rise again." Every one of us that ever lived on the earth. Those who died when they were mere infants, and those who lived to be ninety—all will rise again. Those who were buried in graves will rise again, and those who were engulfed by the sea, torn to pieces by an explosion, or consumed to ashes by a fire, will also rise again. Those who went to church, received the sacraments, prayed, and were honest all their lives, will rise again, and those who in life did not listen to the voice of the bells calling to mass will also hear the sound of the last trumpet and rise again. "We shall all indeed rise again" writes St. Paul; "but we shall not all be changed" (I Cor. 15: 51). Ah, that is it. Only the bodies of the saved will be glorified, those of the damned will be loathsome.

4) You say there is no hell? Then you think in a childish way about God. However frightful hell is, we understand it if we know God's other works.

Here around us is the universe. Its magnitude proclaims God's omnipotence. Here before us stands the cross of Christ: the bleeding Christ upon it proclaims God's boundless mercy. Here before us lies heavenly bliss: it proclaims God's infinite goodness. But here stands hell, too; and what does it proclaim? It proclaims God's infinite justice.

God's justice must be so strict because His omnipotence in the world, His mercy on the cross, and His goodness in heaven, have shown themselves so great. If all these are not sufficient to convert us, what remains? Only His infinite justice in hell.

As the greatness of the world is beyond all our imagination, as the cross is merciful beyond all our hopes, as the boundless bliss of heaven is beyond all our premonitions; so hell is more dreadful than anything we can fancy. And if what St. Paul writes of the happiness of the saved is true, namely, "that eye hath not seen, nor ear heard, neither hath it entered into the heart of man, what things God hath prepared for them that love Him" (I Cor. 2: 9), then it is true of the tortures of the damned that eye hath not seen, nor ear heard them, and the punishment prepared by God for them who do not love Him exceeds all human imagination.

Now I understand how right St. Augustine was when he said that to be separated from God is as great a punishment as the greatness of God Himself (*City of God,* Bk. II, chap. 4).

Imagine an eternal thirst for infinite beauty, for God, and nothing to assuage it. Imagine an eternal hunger for infinite goodness, for God, and not a morsel to satisfy it. Imagine an eternal longing for infinite perfection, for God, and no realization that satisfies it.

There is no friendship, no love, no consolation, no relief, no hope; but there is bitterness and self-accusation, there is reproach and self-laceration, there is abhorrence and regret, but a late regret. Where is the fire that could burn like this? When the lost see the error of their whole misspent lives, but they see it too late.

II

HELL IS ETERNAL

Here we have arrived at the most difficult part of the question. Christianity not only teaches that there is a hell, but also that it lasts forever, that it will never have an end. This is one of the most difficult points of all our religious doctrines; this is one of the greatest stumblingblocks to those not quite conversant with their faith.

A. Eternal hell. Some individuals believe everything else, but here they come to a standstill. The infallibility of the pope they are ready to accept, also the Blessed Mother's virginity: everything but this.

"It is a dreadful thought," they say. "Forever. To live damned forever. Irreparably, irretrievably, hopelessly, forever. No, hell cannot be eternal. For the sin of a few minutes, would the dear God punish in this way?"

1) Truly, our human way of thinking is afraid of the thought. We shudder at it. It is no wonder that we should like to escape from this truth; it is comprehensible that we should like to explain that this is not so: but in vain. This is such a positive teaching of Christianity that there is no doubting it. The same Scripture that speaks of the good God, and of the merciful God, and the gentle and lowly Christ, speaks also of the worm that dieth not and of the fire that is not extinguished (Mark 9: 45). The same Christ who recounted the parable of the father who forgave his prodigal son, also related the parable of the heartless rich man who went to hell and suffered dreadful torment there.

You say hell cannot be everlasting. But then there is no reason for Christ's sacrifice, for His crucifixion. God never does anything without a reason. Yet if hell is not everlasting, then He gave His only begotten Son as a sacrifice without a reason.

If hell is not everlasting, then the martyrs, who died for their faith to insure themselves against eternal perdition, died without a reason. If hell is not everlasting, then it was without a reason that the Apostles and missioners exerted themselves to save the pagans from eternal perdition.

If hell is not everlasting, then there is no meaning in our Lord's memorable words: "If thy hand or thy foot scandalize thee, cut it off and cast it from thee; it is better for thee to go into life maimed or lame, than having two hands or two feet, to be cast into everlasting fire. And if thy eye scandalize thee, pluck it out and cast it from thee; it is better for thee having one eye to enter into life, than having two eyes to be cast into hell fire" (Matt. 18: 8, 9).

Truly, dear brethren, either we must accept this religious truth, that damnation is everlasting, or we must blaspheme by saying that God is not wise in His ways.

2) You say hell cannot be everlasting because "a good God cannot be so severe as to punish a moment's sin eternally." Many try to reassure themselves in this way. But how foolish they are! God's goodness is not helpless weakness or sentimental soft-heartedness. God is really good; but He is also holy and just.

God is good. Yes, good and merciful while we live and strive to turn to Him. Certainly He said: "If your sins be as scarlet, they shall be made as white as snow; and if they be red as crimson, they shall be white as wool" (Is. 1: 18). But all this is only as long as we are in this life. For, after all, God's goodness cannot be weakness and sentimental softness.

Whoever knows what eternal bliss is—the attainment of our spiritual maturity and participation in the life of the God-head—knows that to enter into it is something impossible for those who have spent their earthly lives with their hearts turned away from God.

"For sin lasting but a moment can there be everlasting punishment?" The magnitude of sin is not decided by the length of its duration. It takes only a moment for the murderer to fire his fatal shot. It takes only a moment for a person to lead another into serious sin, for which he may lose everlasting happiness.

It would be more logical to reason in this way: because God is so holy, because sin is in such contrast to Him, hell must be dreadful. Are you truthful? Then you abhor a lie. Are you pure in heart? Then you turn from moral filth. Are you honest? Then you avoid dishonesty. As God is infinitely holy, sin in His sight is infinitely awful, and so by His very nature He must turn from it—forever.

The soul that is in grievous sin at the moment of death—we can say, the soul that dies with heart turned from God—will remain like that for thousands of years, for millions of years, for all time.

Mortal sin is turning away from God a hundred and eighty degrees. Whoever dies like that, whose head stiffens in that position, will remain like that forever: and to live eternally turned away from God is perdition. This is indeed a terrifying doctrine, but it is a sad truth.

B. However, we relieve the awfulness of the belief in hell —we might say we draw the poison-fang from the problem —and our disturbed souls become calmer if we remember that the just God condemns no one to hell who does not deserve it.

1) God does not judge precipitately or under the influence

of passion or at the very moment the sin is committed. He does not judge anyone before He has mercifully called him to repentance and given him a chance to turn over a new leaf. But he who is unwilling to repent, he who does not want to turn to God; what shall God do with him?

War is called the last resort. This is the people's last weapon. They turn to it only when they have tried every other method. Hell is also such a last resort in God's hand. He does not turn to it until He has tried every means of saving us.

It is so little, so incredibly little that God has stipulated for forgiveness. I regret that I was wicked, I promise never to repeat my offense and to confess as soon as possible: that is all. Could He require less than that?

2) Hell, it is true, is a dreadfully formidable doctrine of our faith. But let us consider who goes to hell. He who dies in mortal sin, without confession or, if there was no opportunity for confession, without full repentance, at least.

Mortal sin. Who commits mortal sin? He who deliberately commits a grievous offense against the law of God, after adequate reflection. Thus we know what mortal sin is objectively.

We do not know, however, and no one but God knows, in a concrete case whether a certain person's deed was in reality, also subjectively, mortal sin, although outwardly it appears to be that. We do not know to what extent inherited, perverse inclinations, a neglected up-bringing, evil surroundings, and a thousand other mitigating circumstances may modify the verdict of the all-knowing God.

3) The thought of hell is dreadful, but we are comforted if we reflect: who is there? What does our holy religion teach about this: who is in hell? We do not teach that a single person is there besides the fallen angels and Judas.

There have been monsters in universal history, yet we do

not know for certain whether they are there; on the contrary, there was an executed criminal, the good thief, of whom we know that on the day of his death he reached heaven. Yet according to our human judgment, we would have sent him to perdition, because we judge by the outward seeming. But when God judges He places everything in the balance, every factor that is invisible and incalculable to us, all taint, evil inclinations, a neglected education, wicked surroundings. God puts all these in the scales when He judges. And therefore we do not know who goes to hell.

C. Do not let us rack our brains about who is sent to hell, but rather about how we ourselves may avoid it. We avoid hell if we avoid mortal sin or, if we have had the terrible misfortune to fall into it, if we erase sin from our souls by sincere confession.

1) It is interesting to watch the crowd at a large railway station. What bustling excitement! When the waiting-room doors open everyone rushes to the train, perspiring under their luggage and parcels, pushing and thrusting one another aside. Only one thought possesses them: not to lose the train!

The signal is given, a whistle blows, the crowded train starts. Just then a late passenger rushes on the platform. His hair is dishevelled, his forehead bathed in perspiration, panting and choking he comes to a halt and disappointment rings in his voice as he looks after the departing train and says: "I have missed it."

My brethren, let us bear this in mind when we think of life everlasting. When the train starts for heaven let us not miss it. If we miss it, there is no other train. We have lost it forever.

2) Forever? Again that startling word. I am shaken by it; but I must believe it. My limited human view cannot fully

grasp it, but I believe and declare that God is not stricter with us than we deserve. And I declare that if God's merciful love did not wish to weaken to helplessness, and if God did not wish to expose the moral exertions of honorable, respectable persons to the derisive laughter of the frivolous and light-minded, then He had to create everlasting hell.

If hell were to end, then there would be an end to all serious moral order. The earnest moral efforts necessary to earthly life would at once disappear. Why should I be honorable, why should I hold to my principles, when it does not matter much if I fall?

If there is no omnipotent Judge who will call us to account for the inmost thoughts of our hearts; if there is no judgment seat where all the good deeds we did in secret, all our words, all our heroic struggles will be placed in the balance; if there is no Judgment Day whose effulgence will place the heroism of a virtuous life and the frivolity of light-minded dissipation in their true light: if all this is not, then who can speak of a just, good, and holy God?

Therefore, however dreadful the thought of hell may be, let us all heed its warning. Brethren, endure, persevere. Even at the cost of hard toil, even at the cost of daily struggle, and even at the cost of ceaseless self-discipline, endure at God's side. Turn toward God. Live turned toward God. And die turned toward God.

My dear brethren. After the Israelites had taken possession of Canaan, they swore a solemn oath to keep God's law, as described so graphically in the twenty-seventh chapter of Deuteronomy. Half the people, six tribes, took up a position on Mount Hebal, a barren mountain strewn with ruins; the other six tribes stood opposite on Mount Garizim, a mountain covered with blossoming meadows and forests. In the valley between the two mountains lay the town of Sichem; there the priests and Levites took their stand beside the ark of covenant. "Cursed be the man that maketh a graven and molten thing, the abomination of the Lord . . . and shall put it in a secret place," came the cry of the priests. And the people's reply thundered forth: "Amen."

"Cursed be he that honoreth not his father and his mother."

"Amen," replied the people.

"Cursed be he that removeth his neighbor's landmarks."

"Amen!"

"Cursed be he that perverteth the judgment of the stranger, of the fatherless, and the widow."

"Amen."

"Cursed be he that secretly killeth his neighbor."

"Amen."

"Cursed be he that taketh gifts to slay an innocent person."

"Amen" thundered the people in answer.

But Moses, after prophesying this scene, then continued to speak of what awaits those who keep God's laws. "Now if thou wilt hear the voice of the Lord thy God, to do and keep all His commandments . . . blessed shalt thou be in the city and blessed in the fields . . . blessed shall be thy barns and blessed thy stores, blessed shalt thou be coming in and going out . . . blessed . . . blessed of God."

We are deeply affected when reading this description. Yet what is it compared to the thunder of the last judgment, when no Jewish priest will say the words of cursing and blessing, but the divine Judge; and no people will answer "Amen," but the angels of God.

"Depart from Me," resound Christ's words. And the angels thunder: "Amen."

"You cursed . . ." And the angels reply: "Amen."

"Into everlasting fire." "Amen."

"Which was prepared for the devil and his angels."
"Amen."

But then the wrath will disappear from Christ's face and with infinite gentleness He will turn to the good:

"Come, ye blessed of My Father"; and from millions and millions of hearts the joyous answer will re-echo: "Amen."

"Possess you the kingdom." "Amen."

"Prepared for you from the foundation of the world." "Amen."

Lord God, I believe that there is a hell, but I also believe that there is a heaven. Grant that I may never see hell, but that I may see and possess heaven forever. Amen. Amen.

XVI

ETERNAL BLISS

AMONG the Kamba negroes of East Africa persists an ancient legend.

Once upon a time, long, long ago, according to the legend, the inhabitants of those parts were very embittered by death's merciless destruction. They sent messengers to all countries of the world, to seek a place where death was not lord, so that all the people should move there. The messengers traveled over the face of the earth for years, wandering from one country to the other. Finally they returned with the calamitous news: We must stay here and die as our fathers died, for a kingdom where death is not master does not exist in all the world.

But it does. There exists a kingdom whose inhabitants live forever, and they live in eternal bliss. There is a place where "death shall be no more, nor mourning, nor crying, nor sorrow" (Apoc. 21: 4). There is a place where men "shall no more hunger nor thirst, neither shall the sun fall on them, nor any heat . . . and God shall wipe away all tears from their eyes" (Apoc. 7: 16, 17).

The kingdom of heaven exists where all God's promises to His faithful children are fulfilled, and wherein the last sentence of the Creed becomes holy reality: "I believe in the resurrection of the body and in life everlasting."

"I believe in God." Thus begins our Creed; the avowal of faith in God. "I believe in life everlasting"; thus it ends, with the gaining of God. We begin with faith and conclude with everlasting life, where there will be no more faith, only knowledge.

With the avowal of eternal bliss the Creed ends, just as with the gaining of eternal bliss the zealous life of a Christian ends. Today we will turn our thoughts to the kingdom of heaven, to the realm of eternal bliss, to our real eternal home and, as far as that is possible here on earth, to endeavor to reply to these questions: Does the kingdom of heaven really exist, and what will heaven be like?

I

DOES HEAVEN EXIST?

The most important question for us now is: How do we know that the kingdom of heaven really exists?

A. For an answer we naturally appeal to our divine Master.

1) If there is no heaven then there is no meaning in Christ's whole life. His entire earthly life, His teaching, and His suffering were to enable man redeemed from sin to attain to the heavenly Father's eternal kingdom.

As we read the Gospels we are impressed by the many times and the many different ways Christ spoke of eternal bliss. On one occasion He says to His disciples that whoever sacrifices all for Him, for His name's sake, "shall receive an hundredfold, and shall possess life everlasting" (Matt. 19: 29).

Another time He prophesies to them that they will be persecuted for His sake, but they shall be glad and rejoice, "for your reward is very great in heaven" (Matt. 5: 12).

Or hear what He says in connection with the accumulation of wealth. "Lay not up to yourselves treasures on earth, where the rust and moth consume and where thieves break through and steal; but lay up to yourselves treasures in heaven where neither the rust nor moth doth consume, and where thieves do not break through nor steal" (Matt. 6: 19, 20).

In numerous parables the Savior speaks of eternal happiness. He speaks of it as His "Father's house" (John 14: 2), as "a hidden treasure" (Matt. 13: 44).

Let us recall the beautiful words that will resound at the last judgment: "Come, ye blessed of My Father, possess you the kingdom prepared for you from the foundation of the world" (Matt. 25: 34). Our Lord's doctrine is so permeated by the belief in eternal bliss that the entire Gospel would have to be denied by anyone who wished to deny the existence of heaven.

2) We can see how different is Christ's way of speaking of eternal life from the way others spoke of it before His coming.

Pagan peoples did indeed expect happiness after death. But, as the religions of these peoples were distorted, so they promised themselves a distorted life hereafter: the heaven of religions that were of the earth earthly, full of sensual pleasures, was naturally itself of the earth earthly and sensual.

Not so the heaven of Christ. There is no trace of earthiness in His heaven. His heaven is not a banqueting table of huge dimensions, it is not eating and drinking, or revelry, or the luxury of the Mohammedan seventh paradise. According to Christ, eternal life is His Father's house; Christ goes beforehand there, and there awaits His faithful children. "In My Father's house there are many mansions. . . . I go to prepare a place for you. And if I shall go and prepare a place for you, I will come again, and will take you to Myself; that where I am, you also may be" (John 14: 2, 3).

In the Christian heaven is indescribable bliss; but it is not the bliss of sensual life. It is such bliss "that eye hath not seen,

nor ear heard, neither hath it entered into the heart of man"
(I Cor. 2:9), as St. Paul writes. But this bliss is not made to
earthly measures and for earthly longings. We can imagine
it only dimly, we can hardly form any idea of it; only those
will see it who once attain to heaven.

B. Will many be there? Who will be there? How many
achieve heaven? What an enticing question. And we cannot
answer it.

1) Nevertheless, even though our Lord Jesus said nothing
explicitly about this particular question, I think it is not unseemly curiosity on our part if, approaching the question
with humble heart, we seek a reply to it.

Thinking in a merely human way, the reply would be that
the greater number of those who are not doomed to perdition, do not enter at once after death into God's kingdom,
but must first mature and do penance in purgatorial fire;
but after a shorter or longer period of penance, they reach
God's kingdom.

That would be the merely human reply. On the basis of
Christian hope and humble trust, however, I think we can
give a much more gladsome answer. Of the man who strove
all his life to do God's will—and there are many such also
today, thank God—of the man who lived an honest, dutiful,
religious life, and often purified himself from sin with tears
of repentance in the confessional, who before his death confessed, received holy communion and extreme unction and
full indulgence combined with the papal blessing—of this
man we are justified in hoping that at the moment of his
death he heard the words that our Lord addressed to the
good thief, to the sinner repenting at the last hour: "Amen I
say to thee, this day thou shalt be with Me in paradise" (Luke
23:43).

What a wise thing it is then to pray daily for a happy death.

Many beg God to give them a happy death. But by a happy death they mean that they may not suffer long and may fall asleep calmly, imperceptibly. It is also permissible to pray for this. But much rather should we pray that we may not die without having received the sacraments; a hundred times greater than all the funeral pomp, than all the forests of flowers and funeral sermons is the consolation if we cross the threshold of death with souls at peace with God.

2) "Consolation." Is this heaven only a comforting picture of the imagination, or is it sacred reality? The reproach is often made to Christianity that it works with "bills of exchange on the hereafter," and that if anyone is overwhelmed by a burden of earthly suffering, if anyone is tormented by the disasters of earthly life, it refers to the just and equalizing satisfaction of the other world.

Dear brethren, if this were only the raising of false hopes, such a reproach could rightly be made to our religion. Every bill of exchange is made of value by the name of someone who stands security. Now do you know who drew up this "bill of exchange on the hereafter"? Do you know who stands surety for it? Someone who Himself knew the trials of this earthly life, who Himself went through every phase of suffering, and, acquainted with all this, encouraged His persevering followers in their sufferings with these words: "Be glad and rejoice, for your reward is very great in heaven" (Matt. 5: 12).

If the name of such a Surety is on the bill of exchange, we accept it. If He encourages us with the reward of life everlasting, who Himself came from that life and came that He might help us to attain it, we follow Him gladly. Therefore we believe steadfastly that eternal bliss, the kingdom of heaven, exists.

II

WHAT WILL HEAVEN BE LIKE?

What will heaven be like? In what does its happiness consist? What shall we do in eternity? These are questions that we should like answered.

What shall we do in heaven? Our reply to that is two brief sentences: we shall see God and we shall possess God. This is eternal bliss. Simple words, but fathomless depths lie behind them.

A. We shall see God.

1) Will that really be a source of infinite bliss? The Christian religion has many beautiful customs and salutations that our forefathers used and loved, but not one touches us so deeply as when laying our dear dead in their graves, before taking final leave of them, we send a last good wish after them into their new lives: *Requiem aeternam dona eis, Domine et lux perpetua luceat eis,* "Eternal rest grant unto them, O Lord, and let perpetual light shine upon them."

Perpetual light. In this is contained everything that we expect in heaven. Where there is light, there is recognition. Where light is eternal, there recognition is eternal. Here on earth there is also light: the light of reason and faith. But here we recognize God only dimly. Here no one can see God. But there we shall see Him as He is.

But is that true? Listen to the words of St. Paul: "We see now through a glass in a dark manner, but then face to face. Now I know in part, but then I shall know even as I am known" (I Cor. 13: 12).

Then what do we expect from heaven? What do we ask for our dear ones who have departed from this life? Why do we endure so steadfastly in the temptations of this earthly life? Why do we hold a lighted candle in our hand at our baptism? Why does one burn at our deathbed? Why are several candles lighted on the altar at solemn functions?

Because we are God's children, children of light. We are souls straining from the depths to the heights, from darkness toward perpetual light. The light that reason gives us is only a pale torchlight. That which faith gives is stronger, but it is not fulness of light. I strive forward, toward perpetual light, toward life everlasting, where I shall see God "face to face."

Can this be true? We have the words of St. John: "Dearly beloved, we are now the sons of God, and it hath not yet appeared what we shall be. We know that, when He shall appear, we shall be like to Him because we shall see Him as He is" (I John 3:2).

2) We shall see God, and in God His works. That will be a panorama, to see the plans of divine Providence which in life we often considered hard and unjust. To see the greatest and smallest figures of world history, the celebrated and the forgotten, but now in their true light, the light they have deserved. To see nature's laws and hidden forces, also those that man has never yet discovered. To see all this in the glow of perpetual light, and never be able to cease looking, and never weary of so doing.

We shall also see the angels and all those who have attained their salvation. "I saw a great multitude, which no man could number, of all nations and tribes and peoples and tongues, standing before the throne and in sight of the Lamb, clothed with white robes and palms in their hands" (Apoc. 7:9). What a gallery! What a collection of pictures! Not the oil paintings of Raphael or Murillo or Titian, but of living souls! How much beauty, how much charm, how much nobility!

3) We shall see God. Shall we fully understand God, all His attributes, the profundity of His very being? Ah, no.

A creature cannot fully understand its Creator, nor the finite the Infinite: the ocean cannot be contained in a glass.

But the soul will see God, and not merely believe. We shall not merely see God's reflection in a glass, as we see it here on earth (I Cor. 13: 12), but we shall see God Himself. See and never cease seeing.

We cannot penetrate the unapproachable depths of God's being, that is, we cannot exhaust God entirely, but everyone can see and enjoy as much of God, they can imbibe as much of Him, as they are able to receive. Everyone will see God in different measure, so everyone's eternal bliss will be different, yet everyone will be infinitely happy, because all will receive as much of God as they are able to receive.

Will eternal bliss not be the same for everyone? No. For each one it will be different. Everyone will receive a different measure of happiness but everyone will be infinitely happy and no one will be envious of the other.

The happiness of every soul will be different just as the stars are different the one from the other (I Cor. 15: 41).

How will this be possible?

Let us imagine a crowded concert hall where Beethoven's Symphony is being given. Everyone enjoys it, but everyone enjoys it in a different degree. Each enjoys it according to the amount of musical appreciation he has acquired.

Here is the great lesson we should learn from these truths. The more we occupy ourselves with God in this life, the more we shall receive of Him in heaven. The more we have allowed grace to permeate us here during our earthly lives, the more will "the light of glory," the "perpetual light," permeate us there.

B. This is our answer to those who, in their human and material way of thinking, bring up all kinds of doubt about heaven.

Modern man is made up of nerves, and his work is a continual planning and activity. Hence we should not wonder that he asks anxiously: What is this eternal bliss, what are we going to do there? Our Catholic faith replies that "we shall see God." But what will that be? Shall we stand like white statues and stare stiffly at God, without any activity? Shall we not be wearied if heaven is that?

1) How instructively the legend of St. Augustine answers this question!

An ancient legend says that three hundred years after the death of St. Augustine, a monk, kneeling in prayer at the great saint's tomb, had a remarkable vision. He saw St. Augustine standing with wondering eyes at the gate of heaven, just about to cross the threshold.

"My father," exclaims the monk, "it is now three hundred years since your death occurred, and now you are standing only at the gate of heaven!"

And St. Augustine replies: "Yes, for three hundred years I have been standing here in amazement and wonder at the happiness of the saved. But now I will cease wondering and enter heaven." How much wisdom is hidden behind the simple words of that old legend!

One of the Church's most brilliant intellects and her greatest saint, Augustine, who wrote many treatises on the most difficult theological questions, and whose genius penetrated the depths of the most complicated problems, this St. Augustine arrives in heaven. And its loveliness, its bliss, and its splendor so far surpass the imaginative power of even this marvelous mind that at the very gate, before entering, he has to wonder and admire for three hundred years.

2) Of course, this is only a legend. Heaven has no gate and steps, no towers and battlements. But the gist and essence of the legend is true: the bliss and beauty of life everlasting

are so wonderful that the most brilliant human intellect, the most vivid imagination, is incapable of picturing them even approximately. Not to speak of exhausting them or of being wearied by them.

Shall we not grow weary of them? Does a mother grow weary of watching her little child for hours at a time? Does an artist grow weary when for weeks he plans and improves and paints the subject he has created in his imagination? Does a scientist grow weary when he racks his brains for years over some unsolved problem?

Yet all the created beauty and all the combined treasure of the world are but insignificant grains of dust, mere fragments, compared with the infinite beauty and richness of the infinite God. All earthly beauty is but a shadow of God's beauty.

3) Thus eternity will hardly be sufficient for us to survey God's works. We look twenty or thirty times at St. Peter's Basilica in Rome, at a splendid view from a high mountain; and we are never satisfied. Then what shall we feel when we see the Creator of all created things? When we see not the Alps, not mountain lakes, but the eternal source of all beauty?

If on earth we wish to see clearly, we need a strong light: sunshine, a reflector, an arc lamp. In life everlasting there is also light—not the sun, not electric light, but "perpetual light," the new grace of God—theology calls it the light of glory—that God radiates upon the blessed that in this resplendence they may see Him.

To see God is to participate in some way in God's blessedness, in His activity, in His life. Such a sight of God will not be wearisome monotony, but rather the most stirring and animating perpetual movement and activity: movement and activity, but without fatigue.

C. The sight of God, however, is only one of the sources

of heavenly joy. There we shall not only see God, but we shall also possess Him.

1) Seeing God there is not the same as seeing something here on earth. Here on earth, however joyously we look at something, however long and however deeply, we only absorb its image and remembrance, but the object itself remains outside of us. In heaven, where we look at God without bodily eyes, we shall not receive His image, but His being will enter our soul, will live in us, as today our inmost thoughts live in us. God will embrace us somewhat as, when we throw ourselves into the midst of the billowing sea, we are enveloped on all sides by the ocean.

Let us reflect on some consequences of this truth. If God, perpetual light, envelops us, then we too become radiant. If God, eternal knowledge, envelops us, then we too shall know all that on earth we sought in vain to know. If God, infinite goodness, envelops us, then all our former loftiest desires will be fulfilled. If God, infinite bliss, envelops us, then all joy that earth denied us will be realized.

2) Or we can express this truth thus: every noble endeavor and desire that lived in us on earth, with an imperfection, incompleteness, and insufficiency that left us unsatisfied, will now become our own in the most perfect consummation.

How little we are understood, how often our actions are misconstrued in life! How many complain, and rightly, that they are not in the position where they can properly develop their talents. Many human lives are broken off in the bud, without blossoming or bearing fruit. Many souls struggle enchained in weak bodies, or lost in the mists of ruined nerves and shattered constitutions. And all these limitations will be unknown in heaven.

In life we ask many questions without obtaining an answer. But the answers will be given in heaven. In life we are tormented with many pains. But all pain is banished from heaven.

3) There is one more special source of heavenly joy: the society of Christ and the saints. What an inexpressible flood of joy will flow over us when we stand close to the Lord Jesus!

Lord Jesus. How often have we uttered Thy blessed, holy name! How often have we called upon Thee in temptation! How often have we looked on Thee in the Holy Eucharist where our eyes saw nothing but bread! But now the time has come for which I have prayed so much: the veil has fallen.

With what devotion people make pilgrimages to the tomb of St. Anthony of Pauda, to that of St. Francis of Assisi, to some ancient picture of the Blessed Virgin! But now we shall be with Mary herself. And with the great saints. What a choice society that will be! There is everything truly noble, great, and beautiful that has ever been on earth.

There are our own dear ones, our parents, our relatives. I scarcely need mention the joy we shall experience upon again joining those from whom we took leave at the mouth of the open grave. Nothing of us that is of value will be lost there. In heaven, love and friendship will not be lost, but will be ennobled and strengthened at the very source of love. Thus indeed we shall meet again.

It will be a source of special joy, I think, to see those who are there through our cooperation, through our merits. It will be unspeakable joy to hear such words as these: "Thank you, father, for bringing me up so strictly: that brought me here." "Thank you, mother, that you set me such a good example, and prayed for me: that brought me here." "Thank you, dear wife, husband, friend. Thank you, dear father confessor. Without your help I should never have attained this eternal blessedness."

Eternal blessedness. What marvelous words! What a lively

hope! What a reassuring promise! The end of every journey, the final subsidence of every struggle, the final meaning of earthly life: eternal blessedness. With what reassuring effulgence it radiates above our dark, winding earthly paths and makes bearable the heavy cross of this "vale of tears"!

Eternal life is perpetual light; this earthly life is a great darkness. What I have said about heavenly life, is no more than when a bit of light from a neighboring room steals into a dark room through the crack of the door and lets us know that the other room is brilliantly illuminated.

What I have said is but human stammering. Where is the human imagination that can picture the blessedness of God's kingdom? That blessedness where an infinitely just God will heal our wounds and dry our tears.

God grant that our souls may some day be thrilled with joy when the heavenly gates are opened to us and our Lord says: "Well done, good and faithful servant, because thou hast been faithful over a few things, I will place thee over many things: enter thou into the joy of thy Lord" (Matt. 25:21).

God grant that on the last day we may be standing at the right hand of Christ and hear His welcoming words: "Come, ye blessed of My Father, possess you the kingdom prepared for you from the foundation of the world" (Matt. 25:34). Amen.

INDEX

Abstract concepts and the soul, 17, 20
Activity, man's desire for eternal, 126
Airplane crash (anecdote), 85
Alexander the Great: burial of, 86; grief of, 43
Aloysius (St.) on earthly actions, 102
Ambrose (St.) on life and death, 130
Anecdotes
  airplane crash, 85
  attainment of immortality, 165
  Augustine, St., 38
  beauty of heaven, 46
  Beethoven, 124, 188
  belief in immortality, 56, 124
  the buried village, 140
  certainty of death, 63
  Charles V of Spain, 165
  chief of police in Paris, 54
  conductor on railway car, 91
  consolation of belief in immortality, 120
  cupola of St. Peter's (Rome), 94
  death, 69
  degrees of happiness in heaven, 188
  dream of Genadius, 38
  drunkenness, 54
  earthly cares, 55
  earthly wisdom, 105
  existence of purgatory, 161
  express train, 31
  Francis Joseph I, burial of, 132
  Francis of Assisi (St.) and the mason, 36
  grave in Hannover, 134
  historian crossing the Nile, 55
  hope of immortality, 48
  house of Gerard Kempis, 63
  influence of mind on body, 21
  instinctive belief in immortality, 45

Anecdotes (continued)
  Italian cemeteries, 129
  Johanna ("Mad"), death of, 21
  last judgment, 178
  late passenger, 177
  life, 35
  life after death, 38
  life's goal, 31
  Louis XIV of France, 73
  Massillon's sermon, 161
  Mazarin, death of, 93
  migration of birds, 45
  missionary and the business man, 100
  oath of the Israelites, 178
  poor man on New Year's Eve, 115
  preparation for death, 87, 93, 177
  "Professor Death," 84 ff.
  purgatory, existence of, 161
  purpose of life, 36
  radio receivers, 19
  railway accident (Paris), 116
  rescue from the grave, 87
  responsibility of life, 91, 100
  restraint of belief in immortality, 53
  resurrection from the dead, 134
  Rhone river, 69
  shopkeeper and the sailor, 77
  Socrates, death of, 7
  soldier on battlefield, 3
  soul and the brain, 19
  suffering with Christ, 140
  Tamina Gorge, 35
  Thomas More in prison, 56
  thought of death, 51
  time of death, 77
  tomb of the Hapsburgs (Vienna), 74
  tomb of the Russian czars, 75
  triumph of death, 73 ff.
  triumph of the Church over death, 94

Anecdotes (*continued*)
Tycho Brahe, 105
unbelieving father, 53
uncertainty of life, 85
value of life, 115 f.
violinist, 46
wheat in Egyptian tombs, 120
wine in spring, 48
Zeno and the oracle, 51
Atheists, death of, 42
Augustine (St.)
appearance of (legend), 189
on death, 84
on the death of St. Monica, 164
on eternity, 130
on hell, 172
on possession of God, 52
on the value of time, 105

Baedecker's guide on frescoes, 106
Beethoven (anecdote), 124, 188
Bells of Speyer (German ballad), 131
Berlin National Gallery, 71
Bernard (Claude) on thought, 15
Biology and spiritual phenomenon, 14
Body, resurrection of the, 39
Böcklin: "Isle of the Dead" by, 24; painting of the four ages of life by, 62
Brahe, Tycho (anecdote), 105
Brain: dependence upon the soul, 18; and spiritual creation, 16; and thought, 15
Brevity of life, 109-12
Buried village (anecdote), 140

Campo Santo (Genoa), epitaph in, 34
Cares of the world (anecdote), 55
Change, man's fear of, 97
Charles V of Spain (anecdote), 165
Chinese: belief in immortality among the, 8; emperor (legend), 11
Cholera in Paris (1835), 42
Christ, consolation of the dying by, 148-53
Christian man, Vinet on, 137
Christ's victory over death, 82

Church, consolation of the dying by the, 148-53
Cicero, *De immortalitate animae* by, 7
Clare (St.), Murillo's painting of the death of, 4
Columbus, the courage of, 58
Comfort of death, 129-41
Communion at time of death, 149
Concepts and the soul, 17, 20
Conductor on train (anecdote), 91
Culture, faith the support of, 49-52
Cupola of St. Peter's (anecdote), 94
Czars, tomb of the (anecdote), 75

Danaïdes, punishment of, 168
Dante: on earthly pride, 104; on life and death, 5, 138
Death
Augustine (St.) on, 84
the beginning of immortality, 154
of believing Catholics, 144
the certainty of, 72-76
Christ's victory over, 82
the comfort of, 129-41
the day of compensation, 138
the end of suffering, 130-33
gate to immortality, 58-70
the guide of our life, 119-28
judgment after, 67
the justice of, 131
life's regulator, 5
man's fear of, 95
man's nearness to, 110
man's victory over, 142-53
necessity of preparation for, 92
not a respecter of persons, 64, 132
the painfulness of, 91
passing from life into, 65-70
the passing of honors with, 73 ff.
priestly consolation at the time of, 66
purpose of (anecdote), 69
the regulator of life, 108-18
of Socrates (anecdote), 7
a source of energy, 121
spiritual condition at the time of, 78
the teacher, 84-96
those vanquished by, 143 ff.

Death (*continued*)
  those who vanquish, 144-48
  the thought of (anecdote), 51
  triumph of, 73 ff.
  triumph of the Church over (anecdote), 94
  vanquished by Christ, 147
  the victory of, 21-24, 71-83
  the warning of, 97-107
  warning of our duty by, 102-7
  warning to the ungrateful by, 102
Degrees of joy in heaven (anecdote), 188
Desmoulins, death of, 42
Drunkenness (anecdote), 54
Dürer, "King Death" by, 144
Duty, death's warning of our, 102-7
Dying, Christ's aid to the, 148-53

Egyptians, belief in immortality, 7
Elizabeth of Hungary (anecdote), 75
Epaminondas on greatness, 138
Epitaph: in the Campo Santo (Genoa), 34; of Gardonyi, 7; of Newman, 44; of Veuillot, 2
Eternal bliss; *see* Heaven
Eternal life; *see* Immortality
Eternity, St. Augustine on, 130
Eternity of hell, 173-80
Everlasting life; *see* Immortality
Express train (anecdote), 31
Extreme unction, 149 ff.
Ezechias (King), death of, 60

Father, unbelieving (anecdote), 53
Fear of death, St. Hilary on, 138
Felix (Governor) and St. Paul, 54
"Fidelio," Beethoven's opera, 124
Francis of Assisi (St.): death of, 4; "Hymn to the Sun" by, 138; illness of, 111; and the mason (anecdote), 36
Francis Joseph I, death of (anecdote), 132
Future life; *see* Immortality
Future, our knowledge of the, 89

Gardonyi: epitaph of, 7; on the possession of God, 52

Genadius, dream of (anecdote), 38
Genoa, Campo Santo at, 34: memorials in, 81
Good works, value of, 94
Goodness, immortality demanded by divine, 30
Grave in Hannover (anecdote), 134
Gregory (St.) on the passing of time, 116

Happiness: degrees of heavenly, 188; man's need of, 30; man's search for, 42; in the service of God, 114; and wealth, 105
Happy death, prayers for a, 184
Hapsburgs, tomb of the (anecdote), 74
Hardships of life, 123-28
Heaven, 181-93
  beauty of (anecdote), 46
  belief in, among pagans, 183
  consolation of the belief in, 185
  degrees of happiness in, 188
  the existence of, 182-85
  the joys of, 183
  the nature of, 186-93
  possession of God in, 191
  reunion in, 192
  sight of God in, 190
  society of the saints in, 192
  teachings of Scripture about, 182
Hebbel, death of, 105
Hell, 167-80
  Augustine (St.) on, 172
  the eternity of, 173-80
  the existence of, 168-73
  the justice of an eternal, 174
  necessity for a, 168
  the pains of, 172
  persons in, 174
  teachings of Scripture about, 170
Hell, belief in: difficulty of, 167; among pagans, 168; reasonableness of, 169
Hilary (St.) on fear of death, 138
Historian crossing the Nile (anecdote), 55
Holy Communion at time of death, 149

Honors: object in life, 37; passing of, with death, 73 ff.; St. Philip Neri on, 56
Horace: on life and death, 143; on literary fame, 11
House of Gerard Kempis (anecdote), 63
Hugo (Victor): on life and death, 44; on the powers of the soul, 22
"Hymn to the Sun" by St. Francis of Assisi, 138

De immortalitate animae by Cicero, 7
Immortality
    attainment of (anecdote), 165
    death the beginning of, 133-41, 154
    death the gate to, 58-70
    demanded by God's goodness, 30
    demanded by God's justice, 29 f.
    the existence of, 9-11
    fulfilment of justice in, 41
    God's plan in, 29-32
    hope of (anecdote), 48
    the importance of, 2-5
    instinctive belief in (anecdote), 45
    lack of belief in, 4
    man's search for, 11
    Pascal on, 3
    Socrates on, 22
    teaching of Christ on, 25-29
Immortality, belief in, 1-11
    by ancient pagans, 7
    among the Chinese, 8
    Cicero on, 7
    consolation of, 5, 32, 60, 120 (anecdote), 122
    as a cultural support, 49-52
    Doctor Maye on, 5
    by Egyptians, 7
    encouragement in suffering, 56-59
    the fruits of, 48-59
    man's victory over death by, 142-53
    in prehistoric times, 6
    by primitive peoples, 8
    reasonableness of, 35-47
    regulator of passions, 56
    restraint of (anecdote), 53
    by Socrates, 7

Immortality *(continued)*
    soldier on battlefield (anecdote), 3
    spirit of self-sacrifice from, 53
    strength in temptation, 53-55
    strength in trials (anecdote), 124
    testimony of man's heart, 42-47
    testimony of man's senses, 8
    testimony of man's will, 41 f.
    Thomas More (anecdote), 56
    Veuillot's epitaph, 2
    wisdom of, 9
Instinct, migratory (anecdote), 45
"Isle of the Dead," Böcklin's painting of, 24
Israelites, the oath of (anecdote), 178
Italian cemeteries (anecdote), 129
Ixion, punishment of, 169

Jairus, daughter of, 27
Jo egeszseg, 14
Johanna ("Mad"), death of (anecdote), 21
Joys of heaven, 183
Judgment after death, 67
Justice: of death, 131; of an eternal hell, 174; immortality demanded by, 29 f.; man's desire of, 41

Kamba negroes, legend among, 181
Kempis (Gerard), house of (anecdote), 63
"King Death," Dürer's painting of, 144
Kingdom of eternal life (legend), 181

Labor of Sysiphus, 168
Last judgment (anecdote), 178
Life
    the brevity of, 109-12
    after death (anecdote), 38
    death the regulator of, 108-18
    the goal of (anecdote), 31
    the hardships of, 123-28
    the nothingness of, 85-88
    purpose of, 36
    the responsibility of, 90-94
    the route of (anecdote), 35
    the transientness of, 126
    the uncertainty of, 64, 76-83

Life (*continued*)
  the value of, 88 ff., 115-18
  various views of, 120-23
Life and death: Dante on, 5, 138; Horace
  on, 143; Michelangelo on, 44; St.
  Ambrose on, 130; Victor Hugo
  on, 44
Life everlasting; *see* Immortality
Literary fame, Horace on, 11
Logic, the powers of, 17
Louis XIV of France (anecdote), 73

Massillon, sermon of (anecdote), 161
Materialism and existence of the soul, 12
Maye (Doctor) on belief in immortality,
  5
Mazarin, death of (anecdote), 93
Memorials in cemetery at Genoa, 81
Michelangelo: on life and death, 44;
  statue of St. Peter by, 17
Mind, influence on the body (anecdote),
  21
Missionary (anecdote), 100
Monica (St.), Augustine on the death of,
  164
More (Thomas) in prison (anecdote), 56
Mortal sin, knowledge of, 176
Mourning, Christian way of, 146
Murillo, "Death of St. Clare" by, 4

Nature of heaven, 186-93
Navigius at death of St. Monica, 164
Nervous lady on train (anecdote), 91
New Year's Eve, poor man on (anec-
  dote), 115
Newman: epitaph of, 44; death of, 4; on
  resurrection, 58
Nietzsche on dying, 143

Oath of the Israelites (anecdote), 178

Pagans: belief in hell, 169; belief in
  immortality, 7; belief in purga-
  tory, 157
Pains of hell, 172
Paris, chief of police in (anecdote), 54
Pascal on immortality, 3

Passenger, late (anecdote), 177
Past, our loss of the, 88
Paul (St.) on the resurrection, 28, 57
Paul's imprisonment at Caesarea, 54
Perdition; *see* Hell
Peter (St.), Michelangelo's statue of, 17
Pharaohs, death of the (anecdote), 73
Philip Neri (St.) on worldly honors, 56
Philosophy, Socrates on, 22
Pisa, frescoes at, 142
Plato on the death of Socrates, 22
Pleasure, object in life, 37
Possession of God: Gardonyi on, 52; in
  heaven, 191; St. Augustine on, 52
Prayers for the dead, Tertullian on, 156
Prehistoric man, belief in immortality, 6
Pride, Dante on, 104
Priest, needed by the dying, 66
Primitive tribes, belief in immortality, 8
"Procession of Death," Spangenberg's
  painting of, 71
"Professor Death" (anecdote), 84 ff.
Preparation for death, 92: (anecdote),
  87, 93, 117
Purgatory, 154-66: corollaries to the doc-
  trine of, 160; nature of, 158 ff.; pur-
  pose of, 158; warnings of, 163
Purgatory, the existence of, 155-58: pa-
  gan belief in, 157; and reincarna-
  tion, 162; teachings of Scripture,
  155; teachings of tradition, 156

Radio receivers (anecdote), 19
Railway accident (anecdote), 116
Reason and existence of the soul, 15-23
Reincarnation and purgatory, 162
Rescue from the grave (anecdote), 37
Responsibility of life (anecdote), 91, 100
Resurrection: of the body, 39; from the
  dead (anecdote), 134; Newton on,
  58; St. Paul on, 28, 51
Reunion in heaven, 192
Rhone river (anecdote), 69
Romans, fear of death among the, 86

Sacraments, comfort to the dying, 149 f.
Science and existence of the soul, 13-15

Self-consciousness, 18

Service of God, happiness in the, 114

Shopkeeper and the sailor (anecdote), 77

Sight of God in heaven, 190

Socrates: death of, 22, 145; on immortality, 22; on philosophy, 22

Society of the saints in heaven, 192

Soldier on battlefield (anecdote), 3

Sorrows of death (anecdote), 129

Soul: and abstract concepts, 17; control over the body, 21; dependence upon the brain, 18; spontaneous activity of the, 20; Victor Hugo on powers of the, 22

Soul, existence of the, 12-23: and abstract concepts, 20; attitude of reason, 15-23; attitude of science, 13-15; and materialism, 12

Spangenberg, "Procession of Death" by, 71

Speyer, bells of (German ballad), 131

Spiritual condition at time of death, 78

Spiritualism, 163

Spontaneous activity, 20

Suffering with Christ (anecdote), 140

Sysiphus, labor of, 168

Tamina Gorge (anecdote), 35

Tantalus, torments of, 168

Tertullian on prayers for the dead, 156

Thanks to God, 102

Theseus, punishment of, 169

Thought: and the brain, 15; Claude Bernard on, 15

Time: St. Augustine on the value of, 105; the transitory nature of, 98-100; value of (anecdote), 116

Torments of Tantalus, 168

Transientness of life, 126

Trappist Order, 164

"Triumph of Death," painting at Pisa, 142

Truth, man's desire for, 44

Tytius, punishment of, 169

Uncertainty of life (anecdote), 85

Undertakers, convention of, 61

Value of life, 115-18

Veuillot, epitaph of, 2

Vinet on Christian man, 137

Violinist (anecdote), 46

Warning of death, 97-107

Wealth: the danger of, 113; and happiness, 105; as an object in life, 37

Wine in spring (anecdote), 48

Wisdom, earthly (anecdote), 105

Zeno and the oracle (anecdote), 51